Sociology Transformed

Series Editors
John Holmwood
School of Sociology and Social Policy
University of Nottingham
Nottingham, UK

Stephen Turner
Department of Philosophy
University of South Florida
Tampa, FL, USA

The field of sociology has changed rapidly over the last few decades. Sociology Transformed seeks to map these changes on a country by country basis and to contribute to the discussion of the future of the subject. The series is concerned not only with the traditional centres of the discipline, but with its many variant forms across the globe.

Janneth Aldana Cedeño

Sociology in Colombia

palgrave
macmillan

Janneth Aldana Cedeño
Departamento de Sociología
Pontificia Universidad Javeriana
Bogotá, Colombia

ISSN 2947-5023 ISSN 2947-5031 (electronic)
Sociology Transformed
ISBN 978-3-031-39411-9 ISBN 978-3-031-39412-6 (eBook)
https://doi.org/10.1007/978-3-031-39412-6

This Palgrave Macmillan imprint is published by the registered company Springer Nature Switzerland AG.
The registered company address is: Gewerbestrasse 11, 6330 Cham, Switzerland

Paper in this product is recyclable.

CONTENTS

About the Author

Janneth Aldana is a sociologist, with a master's in Sociology and a PhD in History from the Department of History of the Universidad Nacional de Colombia, in the line of research on historical-genetic studies. The central themes of inquiry revolve around the sociology of culture (specifically the arts) and the sociology and history of knowledge. She belongs to the research group Culture, Knowledge and Society of the Faculty of Social Sciences, Department of Sociology of the Pontificia Universidad Javeriana, where she is also an associate professor.

CHAPTER 1

Introduction

Abstract This introduction presents, in a general way, a journey through the sociological work in Colombia with emphasis on the process of its academic institutionalization at the higher level. Without a strictly chronological order, the aspects that particularize sociology in Colombia are highlighted, facing the national socio-political context but with unavoidable references to the region and the global situation of the mid-twentieth century, when this institutionalization occurred.

Keywords Colombia • Sociology • Institutionalization • Academic field

The chapters that make up this document give an overview of a brief history of sociology in Colombia, with emphasis on its process of academic institutionalization towards the middle of the twentieth century. Although this is only one aspect of such history, because certainly sociological work exceeds the limits of universities, in the Colombian case, institutionalization has been the axis on which production in the area has revolved to this day.

Establishing this process as a starting point, the chapter entitled *Early Experiences* addresses the immediate background that made possible the opening of the first training programs in the discipline at a higher level.

J. Aldana Cedeño, *Sociology in Colombia*, Sociology Transformed, https://doi.org/10.1007/978-3-031-39412-6_1

The ways in which the concern for sociological thought is expressed are directly related, in their beginnings, with the concern about the constitution of the nation after Independence. At the end of the nineteenth century, sociology became the ideal mechanism for understanding the social dynamics that could shape a new social order.

Object of deep debates, this proto-sociology was promoted due to the intellectual production of men linked to law, politics or the media, public figures who had the spaces to propagate their ideas in a still fragile academic-research environment. The close relationship with positivism provided the basis for the first discussions that came to light through essay work, rather than scientific. As a feature shared in several countries of the region, this trend was later called "school sociology".

In relation to the developmentalist perspective that spread throughout Latin America in the first third of the twentieth century, some institutions that were created to leverage this "progress" served as disseminating places for discursive practices close to the social sciences. From state agencies, the establishment of research and study centers that cemented the incorporation of the sociological viewpoint was promoted. To understand their logic, this chapter deals with central aspects of the social, economic, political and cultural conformation of mid-century Colombia.

In the *Academic Institutionalization* chapter, as its name indicates, the exploration focuses on the creation of different university formation programs in sociology. The detailed description around the three pioneering experiences, corresponds to the understanding of the actions carried out by a specific group of people in setting the limits of the discipline, propitiating the conditions of possibility for its development and, fundamentally, establishing the necessary dialogues and spaces to fulfill what, at the time, was understood as its social function. In sum, it exposes the effort made to shape the field of sociology in Colombia and then gain the autonomy necessary for its practice.

Amid the profound politicization brought about by the dynamics of the Cold War, which in Latin America will be felt with all its weight in the transition from 1960 to 1970, the self-reflective exercises that led to the transformation of the initial orientations of the discipline are analyzed. The system of restricted democracy in the country, supported by the form of government called the *Frente Nacional* (National Front), also led to other forms of social organization from which the role of sociology was rethought. Without being able to abandon the problematic around violence, this section closes with a general exposition of the thematic diversity of contemporary sociology in Colombia, paying special attention to the processes of regionalization in this field.

One of the greatest contributions in this reflection appears in the next chapter. The interest in the role of Catholic cooperation networks initially corresponded to the attempt to understand the reasons that led denominational universities to open two of the first three formation programs in sociology in the country. Through this investigation, a whole network was found that was essential for the development of the social sciences. Of course, this is not strange given the weight of an institution like the Catholic Church in Latin America. What is unknown is why, in most regional histories of sociology, this aspect has not been examined with the depth it deserves.

In the chapter *Church, State and Academia*, the reflection however goes beyond the exposition on the incidence of these networks. Specific attention is paid to the primary convergences between the Church's social action and Christian thought, especially that cemented in the *aggiornamento*, proper to the Second Vatican Council. In Colombia, a figure like that of Camilo Torres Restrepo is emblematic in the face of the contradictions that were appearing between this thought and the constitution of a scientific sociology but, mainly, an engaged one. Amid the legitimacy that the revolutionary path had gained at the time, the image of sociology was marked by the weight of events that developed during this period.

This journey closes with an exposition of certain trends that have marked the development of Colombian sociology, while it presents some of the challenges derived from the post-agreements (Havana Agreements—2015—and Cartagena Agreements—2016) and what today is proposed as the Paz Total (Total Peace) project. On the trends, the line marked by the so-called "violentologists" and, in general, the work carried out in the framework of the Colombian armed conflict, whose temporality runs parallel to that which has hosted the trajectory of sociology itself in the country, is highlighted.

Another of these trends corresponds to *Investigación Acción Participativa—IAP—*(Participative Action Research), methodology and epistemology of wide diffusion in Latin America. The figure of Orlando Fals Borda, which appears throughout all the chapters, marks here a turning point that gathers the discussions, still present, between the strengthening of the sociological exercise and what is expected to be its social impact. In view of this, the chapter *Ruptures and continuities in contemporary Colombian sociology* closes with the presentation of a few words on what the author considers to be outstanding current contributions, for their call for attention to aspects that have been neglected and that, therefore, need to be reviewed and expanded within sociology in the country.

The final considerations present a balance of the journey made. These open the discussion on what has so far resulted of the process of historicizing the practice of sociology in Colombia, above all, in the face of the challenges that have appeared for its exercise in different stages. They also propose a small research agenda in relation to central aspects that still need further study.

Among these, it is worth highlighting the need to decentralize research into the different areas that account for the trajectories of the sociological exercise in the country. On the one hand, most sources that address this phenomenon concentrate on the analysis of the case of Bogota and, in this, in the sociology department of the Universidad Nacional de Colombia. On the other hand, sociology goes far beyond the academic sphere, so it is also necessary to investigate other areas in which the profession is developed.

For this book, two researches that try to fill these gaps have been its main support. The first of these corresponds to the project "La institucionalización de la sociología en Colombia. El programa de la PUJ y el Movimiento Cataluña (1959–1972)" ("The institutionalization of sociology in Colombia. The Pontificia Universidad Javeriana's program and the Cataluña Movement (1959–1972)"), carried out between 2019 and 2020. On it, we worked along with Maria Elvira Cabrera, Nicolás Castillo and Ana Camila Jaramillo, sociologists graduated from the Pontificia Universidad Javeriana.

The other research "El campo sociocultural de la sociología colombiana (1960–2010). Un abordaje desde las trayectorias de sociólogos y sociólogas" ("The sociocultural field of Colombian sociology (1960–2010). An approach from the trajectories of sociologists") is currently underway. In it, teachers of various sociology programs in the country participate, myself included. I especially thank Jefferson Jaramillo, who leads the project, and co-researchers Nelson Gómez, Ricardo Barrero, Julián Gómez, Jaime Eduardo Jaramillo and Juan Carlos Zuluaga. For the interviews and reconstruction of trajectories, students of four cohorts of the sociology program of the Pontificia Universidad Javeriana, on the "Sociological Analysis—Colombia" course, have also been collaborators for the construction of this document.

Thanks to these two processes, both funded by the Pontificia Universidad Javeriana, we are making progress in reviewing the existing secondary sources on the subject and the discussions it raises; in the consultation of data from the Archivo Histórico Javeriano (Javerian Historical Archive) and in the development of interviews with sociologists who have been trained and have worked throughout the national territory. Each chapter attempted to give an account of the most relevant sociological production, both for its impact on teaching-learning processes and for its incidence in different spheres.

Professor Stephen Turner encouraged me to present this synthesis in the *Sociology Transformed* collection he publishes with John Holwood. I appreciate the space that he and the collection offer to make this journey known. This effort composes a view that breaks down particular processes and will certainly open up the spectrum of contemporary discussions concerning the global dialogue on the place of sociology in face of contemporary problems. Finally, presenting this publication in English can contribute to the identification of common elements beyond the Ibero-American sphere. Here the accompaniment of Raúl Motta with translation was essential to complete this process.

CHAPTER 2

Early Experiences: From the Sociological Essay to Sociology as Science

Abstract This chapter addresses the transition from an essay perspective around sociology to one that attempted to think of the discipline as a scientific exercise. Particular attention is paid to the socio-political context of the mid-twentieth century as much of the public policies, promoted by the governments in office, allow the comprehension of the initial characteristics of the process of academic institutionalization of sociology in Colombia.

The indisputable predominance of a developmentalist perspective in the analysis of social problems, during the period of interest, was configured from various sources. On the one hand, the influence of North American sociology considered as the best example of scientific scope in the socio-human field. On the other, the good-neighborly programs that amidst the Cold War delineated different kinds of "aid"-political, economic, military, and scientific-.

Due to the historical particularities of the country, those who participated as promoters of the opening of the first training and research centers are part of the so-called "generation of violence". In turn, this was one of the main initial topics of interest, along with its consequences in the urban and rural areas, which occupied the reflective agenda of Colombian sociology.

J. Aldana Cedeño, *Sociology in Colombia*, Sociology Transformed,
https://doi.org/10.1007/978-3-031-39412-6_2

Keywords Sociology • Institutionalization • National Front
• La Violencia

The rise of sociology in Colombia as a relatively autonomous discipline has been dated by most researchers, interested in its history, around the middle of the twentieth century. This classification is based on the recognition that has been made, as a central milestone, of the creation of different educational programs in the area at the level of higher education. Academic institutionalization has been understood as the starting point for the aperture and consolidation of the training, research and social extension spaces[1] that gave entry to sociological work, of a professional nature, to the country.

However, comprehension about any social process can only be found to the extent that the situations or previous circumstances that made it possible and that, in some way, delineated its initial configuration, are considered. In the case of such academic institutionalization, the conditions and dispositions that led a group of people to see sociology as an ideal way to solve certain social problems, explain in broad terms the interest and effort to open social sciences in Colombia.

FOUNDATIONS FOR THE DEVELOPMENT OF SOCIOLOGY

The institutionalization of sociology in Colombia occurred in parallel with similar processes developed by other disciplines in the social sciences. The space opened during the same period for anthropology, geography, or history, corresponded to the attempt undertaken from different public and private instances to find practical and immediate answers to the increasingly evident problems faced by various social sectors in the country. The rapid and abrupt transformations that occurred in the first third of the twentieth century made manifest the need to both understand the new

---

[1] The constitution of any field, in this case the scientific one, is understood from the consolidation of a series of "rules" of operation that are peculiar to it (Bourdieu, 1997, p. 85). In these mentioned spaces, particularly the relationship between research and training, is important to understand the configuration possibilities of a specific knowledge, developed by people who consider themselves experts in it, with the capacity to mobilize resources of various types. The third space, that of extension or social intervention, allows the deepening of the logics of exchange and incidence that far exceed the scientific field itself.

forms of social organization, and to attend to the emerging demands of the less favored sectors, in the face of what seemed an inevitable social conflict.

Nevertheless, since the middle of the nineteenth century, in the face of the process that meant thinking of a post-independence social project, in the midst of a reality marked by the multiple military confrontations that characterized the political construction of the new nation, sociology appeared as the proper field of knowledge to delineate the desired course for the new ruling elites. Without yet calling it by this name, the inquiries that were oriented after the attempt to organize institutionally what was left of the Gran Colombia, related clear sociological concerns through other areas of knowledge moderately consolidated by then.

Examples of this can be found in the works of Manuel Ancizar, Santiago Pérez, José María Samper or Miguel Samper, names that appear as precursors in an effort to understand the social order and explain, from there, what was read as the political instability derived from the need for creation and consolidation of Latin American nations. Among some of the projects carried out during this period, the one implemented by the Comisión Corográfica (1850–1859) must be highlighted, and in it, the role played by Ancizar and Pérez. This commission was the epicenter for observation of the population of the country at all levels (geographical, economic, political, customs and daily life); an observation based on an incipient sociological perspective.

By the end of the nineteenth century several thinkers spoke directly of what, in their eyes, meant the development of a sociological practice. President Rafael Núñez in his first term (1880–1882), closely following the ideas of Herbert Spencer, promoted the entry of sociology into several higher education programs. At his suggestion, Salvador Camacho Roldán obtained the chair of "sociology of the nation" in order to contribute to the construction of a modern liberal state. Famous is his speech where he exposes the general points of the new science: "(...) the one that refers to the laws that, through the social tendencies of man, preside over the historical development of the collective beings called Nationals" (Roldán, 1882, p. 2).

Thus began what could be called a "School Sociology", which focused on discussing the possibilities for the development of the Colombian nation. Other thinkers spoke more about the beginning of an "American sociology", based on the "self-consciousness of a period of historical crisis" (Restrepo, 1980, p. 28), derived from the disintegration of the colonial regime and the opening of an uncertain path to the creation of another social model. However, despite the interest in broadening knowledge around the socio-human sphere that would allow this purpose to be achieved, for this moment they did not yet conceive practical investigations in the field that would make such an expansion possible.

This is considered the first stage of the extension of academic sociology in the country (Cataño, 1986), which coincides with the stage in which the modern social sciences begin in Colombia, due to the creation of certain instances that gradually led to the professionalization of this area of knowledge. The next stage occurs during the so-called Liberal Republic (1930–1946), in which the work of people such as Luis Eduardo Nieto Arteta or Luis López de Mesa stands out, with the linking of a sociological perspective to their studies in law, education or even, in the works of engineering.

Together with new state agencies, such as the Contraloría General de la República (Comptroller General's Office, 1937), studies on the living conditions of certain sectors that had undergone drastic transformations, as had indeed happened with the working class, were advanced. Research and training centers, including the Instituto de Economía de la Universidad Nacional de Colombia (Economics Institute of the National University, 1945), the Departamento de Investigaciones Económicas del Banco de la República (Economic Research Department of the Bank of the Republic, 1944), the Instituto Etnológico Nacional (National Ethnological Institute, 1941) or the Escuela Normal Superior (Superior Normal School, 1935), laid the foundations for the subsequent process of professionalization of sociology in Colombia.

Most researchers point out that, in the case of this discipline, the experience acquired through training at the Escuela Normal Superior—ENS—was fundamental (Leal, 2000, p. 3; Segura & Camacho, 1999, p. 183). There, and at the Instituto Etnológico Nacional, studied people like Orlando Fals Borda himself, Virginia Gutiérrez de Pineda, Darío Mesa Chica, Ernesto Guhl Nimtz, among others, who conformed the first teaching forces for university programs in sociology once they were created, as well as for other programs in the field of social sciences (Jaramillo, 2017, p. 61).

Germán Arciniegas, Luis Eduardo Nieto Arteta and Jaime Jaramillo Uribe were some of the professors of sociology with which the ENS counted. Teaching was given through "introductions" to sociology, study material par excellence, such as those of Armand Cuvillier, Adolf Menzel or Morris Ginsberg. Documents that arrived in the country during these years did so through some periodicals, highlighting the Revista de Occidente, directed by the spanish José Ortega y Gasset, the Biblioteca Sociológica of the argentinian publishing house Losada or the Sociology Section of the mexican Fondo de Cultura Económica (Fund for Economic Culture), under the direction of the sociologist José Medina Echavarría (Jaramillo, 2002).

It was not possible at that time to directly access the material that had already been disseminated in Europe and the United States, between study texts, theoretical documents, or research reports. Moreover, those who were in charge of the first proper classes of sociology had not been trained in the discipline. They were mostly lawyers, philosophers, writers, and intellectuals who, despite these conditions, began to be interested in reaching an empirical inquiry, especially through fieldwork. However, this was the route on which the ground began to be adapted for the arrangement around sociology as a science.

Another fact that supports the search for a proper knowledge of the social sciences in terms of research effort around specific problems, but with the intention of having an impact in various areas through public policy, is the scientific technical assessment exercises hired by different governments. These so-called missions, such as the Currie (1949–1950), the Cepal (1954/1958) and the Lebret (1955) provided novel research models to understand and act on certain social sectors, in an attempt to change Colombian economic policy (Acevedo & Lizcano, 2021). The Lebret Mission, in particular, had an important impact on the development of sociology in Colombia.

Along this path it became evident the need to consolidate a type of approach of a sociological nature, to a reality unexplored so far. The creation of government entities to meet the needs of particular social groups, including the Centro Interamericano de Vivienda (Inter-American Housing Centre, 1941), the Instituto Colombiano de Colonización e Inmigración (Colombian Institute of Colonization and Immigration, 1948), the Departamento de Seguridad Social Campesina (Department of Peasant Social Security, 1953), the Instituto de Crédito Territorial (Territorial Credit Institute, 1939), the Instituto Colombiano de Seguros Sociales (Colombian Institute of Social Security, 1946) (Restrepo, 2002, p. 83), expanded the opportunities for the subsequent professional unfolding of sociologists in the country.

Even so, beyond the space opened in some law, economics or philoso-phy classes, sociology had not found a place dedicated exclusively to its academic-research extension. The first attempt occurred until 1950, with the creation of the Instituto Colombiano de Sociología (Colombian Institute of Sociology) (Restrepo & Restrepo, 1997, p. 7). Made up of professionals from various areas of knowledge, except sociology, perhaps its greatest contribution was the incipient dissemination of disciplinary information along with the beginning of connections with the interna-tional community. This made it possible to achieve a certain breadth of what was hitherto considered a sociological perspective.

The opening of this institute occurred in response to UNESCO's actions to strengthen social sciences globally. Colombia was in fact sce-nario for a congress held in 1956, sponsored by this entity, around the teaching of the different disciplines linked to this field of knowledge. The restrictions that hindered the dissemination of, and training on social sci-ences were evident, especially due to the deficiency or lack of research experiences that would really allow a closer comprehension of the most relevant and urgent social problems (Restrepo, 1980, p. 43).

Although the Instituto Colombiano de Sociología had a short life, it was a manifestation of the growing possibilities for the creation of centers or schools of training in sociology, as well as the need to have professionals in the area in view of the interest of intervening, through "planning", in various social areas. Then began the third stage of this period in the pro-fessionalization of sociology in Colombia, stage which main characteristic was the creation of the first educational programs in higher education.

Colombia in the Mid-Twentieth Century

In the Latin American panorama, Colombia was characterized by being the country that went through an abrupt transformation towards what, at the time, was considered the entrance to "modernity". If the second half of the nineteenth century had been the scene of the inertia inherited from the colony in terms of the link with international trade, that is, in relation to the connection with the world beyond geographical borders; the twen-tieth century opened the doors of the territory, thanks to coffee, in a process that brought rapid changes in social organization.

The conditions for entering the new century were unfavorable for the country in the midst of the last great civil conflict of this period, the so-called La Guerra de los Mil Días (Thousand-Day War) (1899–1902).

With an economy shattered, an impoverished population, mostly rural, in an extremely fragmented territory whose greatest expression had been the loss of Panama, and without a clear project of political leadership after years of conservative party rule, the horizon was not encouraging.

Thus, during the first decades of the twentieth century, precarious economic development prevailed in Colombia. In addition to the high poverty rates, the inhabitants were characterized by high levels of illiteracy without having educational opportunities, which were granted only to men belonging to the elites. However, by the 1920s, the coffee economy became the trigger for an accelerated and profound change, unprecedented in the country's short republican history (Palacios, 1995, p. 128).

Along with the colonization of the central massif of the Andes due to the extension of coffee, the urban centers were consolidated either due to the financial development of the new economic dynamic or to mining, oil and banana exploitation that was being strengthened in some areas of the country. At the same time, workers' movements, as well as those formed by other popular sectors, became more dynamic and exerted greater pressure in the search to improve their working conditions, as well as living conditions for themselves and their families. Under these circumstances, the chances were increased for liberals to return to power in the 1930s.

During the Liberal Republic (1930–1946) a "developmentalist" perspective was favored through which actions were promoted that sought a social impact from above through public policy. This perspective was part of an effort to modernize, from the State, other spheres of society beyond the economic. Thus, areas such as education and culture received unusual attention from political elites. A clear example occurred during the so-called Revolución en Marcha (Revolution on the March), under the first government of Alfonso López Pumarejo (1934–1938), with the reorganization of the Universidad Nacional de Colombia or the creation of the ENS.

The expansion of enrolment in higher education clearly favored the middle class. Although it was not the only one that obtained benefits from the State. The working sectors also received important support with the backing of the creation of unions such as the Central de Trabajadores de Colombia—CTC (Central of Workers of Colombia). The rise of the middle class and the strengthening of various organizational processes were accompanied by higher levels of schooling, industrialization and urbanization. The doubling of the population in the main cities between 1938 and

1951 (Corredor, 1992, pp. 190–193) was perhaps the expression of the most dramatic change in Colombian society during this period.

Although the reformist impulse of various liberal governments had far-reaching consequences in face of the desired social transformation, they proved to be limited. The regime change did not make a dent in a political system that for a long time would be dominated by bipartisanship, with the rotation of power between the liberal and the conservative party. On these parties, national identity was built; an identity that ended up being based on clientelism and that, ultimately, did not allow liberalism and its modernizing intention in economic terms, to lead to longer-term political and social reforms.

However, it is worth highlighting a certain strength of cultural policies during this period, in a country with an indisputable predominance of the Catholic religion in various fields. These policies, aimed at the masses, under a particular vision of the popular from folklore, allowed the development of some research projects with the purpose of knowing the inhabitants of the country and their living conditions (Silva, 2005). The unprecedented rise of some mass media such as radio and film allowed at the same time an opening to international events which, despite resistance, advanced the process of secularization.

The reformist project under the Liberal Republic, in general, received strong opposition from the Catholic Church and the conservative party. From the elites of the country these efforts were countered with relative success, bringing as a consequence the brake to the attempts of organization of the popular bases and the middle class. A fragile State, in the midst of a deeply divided territory, could not integrate the entire Colombian population into the national project that had been proposed from above.

This partly explains why, between the reformist and the developmentalist visions that had been configured during this period, as a strategy to achieve the desired social transformations, the latter ended up imposing itself. The predominant developmentalist vision, not only in Colombia but in Latin America, turns out to be a central aspect when it comes to understanding the development of academic sociology and, in particular, the support it received not only from university directives but, the State through various governmental bodies.

It is important to note that, for the Colombian case during the 1940s, this confidence in developmentalism as a mechanism of social restructuring resulted rather, and not infrequently, in a mechanism that appealed to repression to achieve social regulation. In this way, the country would begin to become accustomed to the use of violence as an immediate response to social conflicts. This, in a society with great divisions, made the idea of a social pact untenable (Pecaut, 1985).

The difficult social conditions of the peasant and working-class sectors were not very encouraging. Without the capacity for dialogue with the ruling elite, made up specially of commercial and industrial groups, these sectors either did not know or could not have a greater interest in achieving that western "modernity" via development management. The small opening and diversification caused by the impulses to industrialization and increasing urbanization had certainly not worked as a mechanism for social mobility.

This process, carried out with the backs of the majority of the population, raised the levels of popular discontent caused by the undeniable inequality. The less favored sectors, affected by this condition, became more active manifesting this discontent. Although in the following years efforts were made to reduce illiteracy (by 1945 it is estimated that 60% of the population could not read or write) with an increase in schools, as well as improving living conditions with the construction of hospitals and other infrastructure to provide basic services (Henderson, 2006, pp. 368–373), social tensions continued to increase.

Additionally, Colombia maintained regional fragmentation. With industrial expansion, three urban centers were consolidated: Bogota, Medellin, and Cali. While in the cities there was an increase in the unionized population, that is, organized with the purpose of claiming their rights, in the countryside the capacity to improve the situation of the peasants did not emerge even as a possibility. This break between the urban and the rural would be one of the factors that will sustain the social and armed conflict in the country for decades.

Both in the cities and in the countryside the patriarchal Catholic social order that had predominated until now, and that, right or wrong, had functioned as a factor of integration, was broken. Under these pressures, it is not surprising the authoritarian response of the elites, a response that gave rise to certain populisms expressed in central political figures of the period such as Laureano Gómez or Jorge Eliécer Gaitán.

The weakening of what had been constituted as regional loyalties based on the extension of the two traditional parties (the liberal and the conservative), in the midst of a capitalist modernization project, explains in part the dramatic reaction of rural violence that, since then, has become evident, with different flows, in the country. During the end of liberal hegemony in 1946 and the return of the conservative, with the parallel disinterest to address the so-called "the social question", the fracture between the urban world of elites and the leaderships that were forming in the countryside led to "*La Violencia*" (The Violence).

With a capital letter, "La Violencia" as a period usually dates from 1946 to 1965, although regional differences sometimes make it preferable to talk more about Las Violencias in plural, which covered much of the national territory. Likewise, although Colombia seems to be a paradigm of democracy in the region, especially because it has never suffered a military coup, it is impossible to miss the violent history that defined its short republican life and that led it, in the nineteenth century, to be the scene of various civil wars (Sánchez, 1991, p. 19).

The reference to this period becomes relevant because, just as it is the moment in which the conditions for the emergence of academic sociology in Colombia were configured, its main promoters are recognized as belonging to the Generation of La Violencia or the Generation of the State of Siege. Due to the deep gulf that eventually opened between the ruling elites and the popular sectors, the country was plunged into a state of terror over which it has been impossible to calculate the effects in loss of human lives (between 100,000 and 300,000) as in material damages, especially in rural areas.

La Violencia showed the gaps between the countryside and the city, which still characterize the country today, as differential scenarios of the armed conflict. Those who bore the brunt of the consequences were the peasants, while the urban elites continued their usual work in the midst of the development of industrial capitalism. As already mentioned, La Violencia had different manifestations according to the territory, but as a common distinguishing feature, it expressed the bipartisan struggle between liberals and conservatives that ended up defining the opposing sides (Pecaut, 1991, p. 262).

One of the events with greater resonance during these years was El Bogotazo. On April 9, 1948, the liberal leader Jorge Eliécer Gaitán was assassinated. A few hours later, not only was part of the city center on fire, but the possibility of a social revolution was also under consideration. This was averted with a quick agreement among the elites and with the identi-fication of communism as the common enemy, as put forward at the time by the conservative president Mariano Ospina Pérez. The hypothesis of communist infiltration was effective in avoiding reflection for a long time on this event. Bogota, during that week, was the headquarters of the IX

Pan American Conference that gave rise to the Organization of American States—OAS—a week in which the young Fidel Castro was also in the Colombian capital (Braun, 1991, pp. 228–229).

After several conservative governments, with the departure of Laureano Gómez in 1953, a military government was established at the head of General Gustavo Rojas Pinilla. Unlike other countries in the region, the new government did not come to power due to a military coup but to an agreement between the same party members. The Rojas administration stimulated a major development of public services in education, health, communication, and transport and, by opening a window for the organization of new political movements, generated a strong reaction among the elites leading them to create a "pact".

The so-called *Frente Nacional* (National Front) (1958–1974) emerged as a coalition that, through the alternation of power between the two traditional political parties, sought to bring "peace". Although it is true that during the first years violence decreased because of bipartisan struggles, soon this system resulted exclusive by cementing a restricted democracy that prevented the rise of new social forces. Under these conditions, sociology appeared as a response to growing social tensions.

TOWARD THE INSTITUTIONALIZATION OF SOCIOLOGY

Under the circumstances described previously, sociology was given a window of opportunity. The first governments of the National Front promoted a series of actions aimed at various sectors of the population, in what was conceived as a democratic reconstruction after the misunderstood period of La Violencia. As a change from above, it was thought about the need to develop public policies elaborated and executed from an expert knowledge.

Not only in Colombia, because it was a shared idea at the regional level, the modernization effort was continuing its course by trying to place Latin America in a less disadvantaged condition at the international level. Among the main promoters of the opening and consolidation of the fundamental spaces for the development of sociology in the country were those who, by the end of the 1950s, considered it as such expert knowledge appropriate for this purpose.

Although in Latin America the academic institutionalization of the discipline responded in part to particular dynamics, as in Argentina in the face of migration and the expansion of the middle classes or in Brazil with the changes brought by industrialization and trade in large cities or multi-culturalism given the country's ethnic wealth, this process presents similar situations in the region. One of the most outstanding dynamics has to do with the effort to develop a "scientific" sociology, with the name of Gino Germani at the head, along with the work of other central figures in the period such as José Medina Echavarría, Florestán Fernández or Luís Álvaro Costa Pinto (Blanco & Jackson, 2015, p. 21).

With a strong influence of North American sociology, by the end of the 1950s, there was a transition from an "essay" sociology, sustained in the work of intellectuals, politicians or journalists, to a scientific sociology, with the creation and strengthening of training and research spaces in social sciences. Some regional centers were key in this process, including the Comisión Económica para América Latina y el Caribe—CEPAL (Economic Commission for Latin America and the Caribbean, 1948), the Facultad Latinoamericana de Ciencias Sociales—Flacso (Latin American Faculty of Social Sciences, 1957) or the Instituto Latinoamericano de Planificación Económico Social—Ilpes (Latin American Institute of Social Economic Planning, 1962) (Roitman, 2008, p. 34).

In the region, the search for the desired political order, after the shared concern around the post-independence national construction, had as its axis since the second third of the twentieth century the idea of "modernization". This is a central issue in understanding the particularities of sociology in Latin America, as well as some elements present in the global south: the colonial past. During this period the problem of having a political-administrative organization, heir to a slave regime, which did not work to take on the new challenges of social mobility, became evident (Vergara, 1997, p. 16).

The image of an underdeveloped Latin America fed this ideal of overcoming the crisis through "modernization". Among multilateral organizations and government initiatives, promotion was given for the strengthening of sociology, for its transition from a sociology of lectures to a scientific one based on social research. Not minor was the role played in this process by the universities themselves, academic-research spaces that provided the basic initial conditions in the configuration of an enabling environment for the "new" science.

The fact that this type of institutions, and in particular the multilateral organizations, gave all their economic and technical support corresponded to the general view typical of the Cold War, to the need to respond expeditiously and effectively to complex social situations. The destabilization of the region, under pressure from various traditionally excluded and marginalized sectors that were beginning to mobilize more strongly, had raised alarms about the solidity of the system defended in the Western Hemisphere.

In Colombia, undoubtedly phenomena such as La Violencia and the attempt at pacification that came from the National Front, with its political, social, economic, and cultural consequences, outlined the first interests towards which sociology was oriented. The need to face the consequences of years of social disintegration, due to the inability to resolve social tensions through non-violent or repressive means, forced the gaze at social sciences.

It has already been mentioned how concerns about high illiteracy, precarious industrialization, the transformation of a rural country to an urban one, among others, led to the constitution of a number of planning agencies to serve specific populations. In such agencies, however, by the end of the 1950s, it became increasingly clear that there was an urgent need to have qualified personnel to know and act on various problems, pending for appropriate results upon them.

Thus, during this period, the need to promote high-level training and research in sociology became evident. Three programs in higher education institutions were pioneers in this attempt, two located in Bogotá, at the Universidad Nacional de Colombia (National University of Colombia) and the Pontificia Universidad Javeriana (Pontifical Javeriana University), and another in Medellin, at the Pontificia Universidad Bolivariana (Pontifical Bolivarian University). At the moment, without other centers of study or research, universities had the basic requirements, at least those related to training in different fields of knowledge.

By that time, the Universidad Nacional de Colombia was the main center of thought, training and research of the country, reason why its classrooms were precursors in housing future professionals in sociology. In the case of universities run by religious communities, interest in this discipline corresponded largely to the work carried out by several of its members, thanks to pastoral work, in communities and neighborhoods throughout the national territory. In addition, until the middle of the twentieth century, if an institution had managed to penetrate all spheres in Latin America beyond its own religious sphere, it was the Catholic Church.

Common Ground

An initial overview of these first three programs offers enough elements to understand the generalized vision that existed in Colombia, around sociology, between 1950 and mid-1960. We must not forget, however, the social context that will define the first outlines of the curricula: from the social changes themselves resulting from the progressive urbanization and its consequences with the transition from a rural country to an urban one; the growing pressure from the workers, peasants, and students sectors; and the subsequent organization of insurgent movements under the strong influence of the Cuban Revolution throughout the region.

As common features, regardless of the character of the university, these programs had as promoters people who had previously been trained in the discipline in European and American institutions. Through an existing network of academic exchanges, some Colombians obtained scholarships to study abroad. It was also usual for specialists to arrive, mainly from the United States, as part of economic aid or technical assistance destined to Latin America.

This is one of the reasons why American sociology predominated during the first years, under the idea of a practical, empirical science, strongly oriented by structural functionalism. It was not only this close relationship with the northern country; this predominance was related to the transitions of the discipline itself given the conditions of the second postwar period and the decline of the main research centers in Europe.

Conceived as a practical science, this sociology was constructed as an area of convergence between academic-research work and its incidence in central areas to which public policy was directed (Jaramillo, 2017, pp. 21–56). From the classrooms it was easy to move to different state offices and ministries, entities in which sociological knowledge was considered an expert knowledge. As already mentioned, the predominant view of the period on the need to modernize the country was the primary incentive for the development of sociology in Colombia.

Thus, although the universities that made possible the opening of the first programs differ by their institutional character (since one of them is public and secular while the other two are private and Catholic), all highlighted support for sociology thanks to the intention to advance national planning processes in areas such as rural reform, housing programs, care for vulnerable populations, among other issues considered central as social problems in the country (Cataño, 1980, p. 54). In this way, sociology was characterized, in its beginnings, by following the paths it opened for social intervention.

In addition to shared interests, these institutions had to confront the same obstacles, facing the configuration of a scientific field. The formation of a suitable teaching staff was not easy because, although many people had expressed their interest in sociology, few had had high quality training or had developed a research trajectory in the area. In addition, the dissemination and teaching material was still quite scarce without the lack of networks or spaces for the exchange of knowledge developed so far, at least not at the national and regional level.

The support provided by governmental bodies and multilateral organizations proved to be essential, especially at the Universidad Nacional de Colombia, in obtaining the necessary resources to overcome these difficulties, resources added to those granted or administered by religious communities, whose transnational network was quite strong in the second half of the twentieth century. For the members of the latter it did not go unnoticed the sociology that, in a certain way, found correspondence with the development of a progressive Christianity that would be strengthened in the 1960s with the Second Vatican Council.

This economic and technical support, coming especially from the United States and Europe, was framed in the aforementioned bet for the "development" of the region based on the tensions of the moment between the capitalist world and the communist world. In addition to agencies supported by the US government such as the United States Agency for International Development—USAID—created by John F. Kennedy, other private ones, including the Rockefeller, Ford and Fullbright, promoted the development of social sciences in Latin America (Picó, 2003).

Along with the promotion of applied research in key sectors such as agriculture, health, and education; exchange between specialists and North-South experts, in particular, and the granting of higher education scholarships for Colombians abroad, the foundations were laid for the creation and consolidation of academic-research spaces specific to sociology.

The First Sociology Programs in Colombia

In 1959, the first three sociology teaching programs were created at the higher level. Among them, the one that had greater recognition at the national and international level, remained open and functioning since it was created, and provided the basis for the extension of the discipline in other universities in the country, was created at the Universidad Nacional de Colombia. The figures that marked the image of the professional in sociology, not only for being pioneers but for what they represented in terms of their national presence in the political and cultural sphere, Orlando Fals Borda and Camilo Torres Restrepo, were also its main drivers.

Fals Borda, trained in sociology at the universities of Minnesota and Florida (United States) and Camilo Torres, graduated from the University of Leuven (Belgium), along with other professionals, built a training program entirely tied to research in sectors that were considered crucial to address the most pressing problems of the moment. In this way, rural sociology and urban sociology occupied the center of the stage with a display of scientific character, attending to the gradual social change, characteristic of the developmental perspectives of the moment.

Along with this research work, professionals who worked as teachers in the Universidad Nacional de Colombia also found their place in the national planning offices, as well as in some ministries. With the support of the Government and international cooperation institutions, they succeeded not only in obtaining the necessary resources to carry out sociological research, they also enabled a way to apprehend the contours of the discipline beyond strictly academic boundaries.

The general guidelines that guided the sociology study program at the Universidad Nacional de Colombia, as well as the research project that was configured during the first years, resulted from the intersection between the effort to advance an empirical and applied sociology, the liberal democratic ideal advocated by the National Front and the progressive Christianity that was beginning to predominate in the region (Jaramillo, 2017, p. 296). This was the same path that was followed at the other two institutions of higher education that created programs in sociology, although with a clear hegemony of the Christian vision of the social order.

As for the sociology programs of the Pontificia Universidad Bolivariana and the Pontificia Universidad Javeriana, also created in 1959, there are no outstanding figures as promoters. What supports these initiatives is the long-standing pastoral work of the Catholic Church in the country. For sociology, this trajectory was fundamental at a time when "the social question" appeared as the main issue to be addressed, derived from the rapid transformations that Colombian society was going through.

"The social question" occupied a central place in the Catholic Church since the late nineteenth century as a way of dealing with what was considered the unintended consequences of capitalist development. This was accentuated in the twentieth century by the spread of communism and the fear it aroused among the political and economic elites, as well as in the church hierarchy, the possibility that the most impoverished sectors saw in this political current, or any other leftist tendency, a possible way out of their conditions of poverty, inequality, and marginality.

In Medellin, derived from the Fifth Colombian Social Week that had been organized by the Archdiocesan Curia in 1958, the Pontificia Universidad Bolivariana proposed the creation of a sociology program that would contribute to the training of expert professionals to address the most obvious difficulties of the country, but from a Christian perspective (Serna, 1996, p. 146). In this way a new discipline was thought that, by then, would not contradict the social doctrine of the church.

As a guarantee of the close relationship between sociology and the Church, the extensive training of professionals of this discipline in Catholic universities appeared. Just as Camilo Torres studied at the University of Leuven, Maria Cristina Salazar, who directed the first years of the sociology program at the Pontificia Universidad Javeriana, studied at the Catholic University of Washington. Salazar had the support of José Rafael Arboleda S.J, who used to represent the country in various national and international events where the development of social sciences was discussed.

Sociology as an applied science dedicated to understanding and contributing to the solution, through concrete actions, of tensions between various social groups, was the predominant vision during this period. For catholic universities, the conviction that this was only possible through expert knowledge, though of course Christian, led to the strengthening of an entire institutional apparatus. This was built on bases existing in the most remote territories of the national geography, bases close to peasants and workers, and on a hierarchy connected to a transnational network from which came important resources that supported the academic institutionalization of sociology in Colombia.

REFERENCES

Acevedo, Á., & Lizcano, L. (2021). Misiones económicas en Colombia y su inci-dencia en la educación técnica industrial (1930–1960). *Revista CS, 34,* 241–264. https://doi.org/10.18046/recs.i34.4193

Blanco, A., & Jackson, L. (2015). *Sociología en el espejo. Ensayistas, científicos socia-les y críticos literarios en Brasil y en la Argentina (1930–1970).* Universidad Nacional de Colombia de Quilmes.

Bourdieu, P. (1997). *Razones prácticas. Sobre la teoría de la acción.* Ed Anagrama.

Braun, H. (1991). Los mundos del 9 abril, o la historia vista desde la culata. In G. Sánchez & R. Peñaranda (Comp.), *Pasado y presente de la violencia en Colombia* (pp. 225–261). Cerec.

Cataño, G. (1980). La sociología en Colombia: un balance. In *La sociología en Colombia. Balance y perspectivas* (pp. 51–81). Memoria del III Congreso Nacional de Sociología. Colciencias.

Cataño, G. (1986). *La Sociología en Colombia.* Editorial Plaza y Janés.

Corredor, C. (1992). *Los límites de la modernización.* Cinep.

Henderson, J. (2006). *La modernización en Colombia. Los años de Laureano Gómez 1889–1965.* Editorial Universidad de Antioquia.

Jaramillo, J. (2002). Notas para la historia de la sociología en Colombia. In G. Cataño (Comp.), *De la sociología a la historia Obras completas de Jaime Jaramillo Uribe* (pp. 29–50). Ceso, Uniandes.

Jaramillo, J. (2017). *Estudiar y hacer sociología en Colombia en los años sesenta.* Ediciones Universidad Central.

Leal, F. (2000). Vicisitudes de la profesionalización de las ciencias sociales en Colombia. In F. Leal & G. Rey (Eds.), *Discurso y razón. Una historia de las ciencias sociales en Colombia* (pp. 1–14). Tercer Mundo.

Palacios, M. (1995). *Entre la legitimidad y la violencia. Colombia 1875–1999.* Norma.

Pecaut, D. (1985). *Orden y violencia 1930–1953.* Cerec, siglo XX ed.

Pecaut, D. (1991). De las violencias a la violencia. In G. Sánchez & R. Peñaranda (Comp.), *Pasado y presente de la violencia en Colombia* (pp. 262–273). Cerec.

Picó, J. (2003). *Los años dorados de la sociología (1945–1975).* Alianza Ed.

Restrepo, G. (1980). El departamento de sociología de la Universidad Nacional de Colombia y la tradición sociológica colombiana. In *La sociología en Colombia. Balance y perspectivas.* Memoria del III Congreso Nacional de Sociología (pp. 21–50). Colciencias.

Restrepo, G. (2002). *Peregrinación en pos de omega: sociología y sociedad en Colombia.* UN.

Restrepo, G., & Restrepo, O. (1997). Balance doble de treinta años de historia. In *La sociología en Colombia. Estado académico* (pp. 3–67). Icfes.

Roitman, M. (2008). *Pensar América Latina. El desarrollo de la sociología latino-americana.* Marcos Roitman Rosenmann. Clacso.

Roldán, S. (1882). *Discurso leído por Salvador Camacho Roldán. Profesor de sociología de la Universidad Nacional de Colombia, en la sesión solemne de distribución de premios a los alumnos, el día 10 de diciembre de 1882.* Imprenta de Echeverría Hermanos.

Sánchez, G. (1991). Los estudios sobre la violencia. In G. Sánchez & R. Peñaranda (Comp.), *Pasado y presente de la violencia en Colombia* (pp. 17–32). Cerec.

Segura, N., & Camacho, A. (1999). En los cuarenta años de la Sociología Colombiana. *Revista de Estudios Sociales, 4,* 23–35. https://doi.org/10.7440/res4.1999.02

Serna, A. (1996). Una mirada a la sociología en Medellín. Balance doble de treinta años de historia. In *La sociología en Colombia. Estado académico* (pp. 145–183). Icfes.

Silva, R. (2005). *República liberal, intelectuales y cultura popular.* La carreta histórica.

Vergara, F. (1997). *Ciento catorce años de la sociología en Colombia.* Sistemas y Computadores Ltda.

CHAPTER 3

Academic Institutionalization

Abstract The purpose of this chapter is to present the process of academic institutionalization of sociology in Colombia, which initiated with the creation of the first programs in Bogota and Medellin in the late 1950s. The following decades were scene for the opening of many other programs and research centers throughout the national territory. This extension not only made it possible to reach other regions; in turn, it expanded the thematic agenda in which the group of professionals trained in the discipline began to specialize.

Without losing sight of international networks, especially those that strengthened their presence in Latin America, the country's particularities defined precise contours in the most prominent research problems. In this manner, the prolonged armed conflict, and the manifestation of various forms of violence during the second half of the twentieth century, became the axis on which the so-called specialized sociologies were articulated. From a perspective that favored direct intervention as a possibility for social change, efforts turned to the search for a critical sociology that would allow reading the reality of the region and the country as part of conflicts at a global level.

Keywords Critical sociology • Professionalization • Armed conflict • Internationalization

© The Author(s), under exclusive license to Springer Nature Switzerland AG 2023
J. Aldana Cedeño, *Sociology in Colombia*, Sociology Transformed, https://doi.org/10.1007/978-3-031-39412-6_3

The first university-level sociology programs began in the late 1950s. By the middle of the next decade, these programs underwent deep changes both in the organizational conditions of the teaching staff and in the research spaces, as in the conception of the theoretical and methodological foundations that had hitherto guided the teaching of the discipline. This is the basis on which the professional field of sociology emerged in Colombia.

The possibilities created by the consolidation of the academic-research environment, together with the expectation of the opportunities it offered for social intervention, early and quickly opened the doors of various institutions and organizations, public and private, to sociology. Classroom teaching thus not only found ground for "application"; it also placed future professionals in key spaces of the definition and development of public policy. This undoubtedly was the central support for the rise of sociological work in various parts of the national territory.

OVERVIEW OF THE FIRST PROGRAMS

Between 1959 and 1967, new training programs in sociology were created and existing ones in Bogota and Medellin were strengthened. In particular, the teachers and students of the Universidad Nacional de Colombia, with their research commitments and their presence in government agencies, set the tone for what would be the development of sociological knowledge during this period in the country. At the same time, participation in important events, at least at the regional level, opened the dialogue with other schools and researchers in Latin America.

In an early manner, the Faculty of Sociology of this university joined the Asociación Latinoamericana de Sociología (Latin American Sociology Association)—Alas, an organization that had been created in 1950 (Vergara, 1997, p. 47). As part of its activities, the organization of the IV Latin American Congress of Sociology (1964), based in Bogota, was in charge of Orlando Fals Borda and Camilo Torres. The way the event was coordinated illustrates the interest in strengthening a Latin American sociology that, however, needed resources from the public and private sector, external to the region, for its financing and in general terms for its institutional take-off.

For this event, the different national associations of sociology summoned about 317 delegates, among which some personalities of Latin American, North American and European sociology stood out. Jorge

Graciarena, Pablo González Casanova, Aníbal Quijano, Aldo Solari, Françoise Houtart, Talcott Parsons, among others, met in Bogota (Parra, 1975, pp. 29–30) with the central support of the Rockefeller and Ford Foundations, and USAID (Jaramillo, 2020, p. 117).

With it all, the trajectory followed by Colombian sociology during this first decade can be traced, in part, through the dynamics of the first national congresses. Convened by the Asociación Colombiana de Sociología (Colombian Association of Sociology), an organization founded in April 1962 with the aim of protecting sociologists as a professional group, strengthening social research in national territory (Cataño, 1980, p. 52) and expanding the academic and cooperation networks of various entities, the congresses allow to delve the transformations of the discipline in the country.

In March 1963 the First National Congress took place. Presided by Camilo Torres Restrepo, it collected lectures ranging from the issues of sociology teaching to the problem that became central to the first research projects in the area: rural violence and the agrarian question. In this space it was also clear the purpose of delimiting the boundaries of sociological work, compared to other very close ones, such as social work. As articulating axis, it was insisted on the need to develop a science that would allow the comprehension and promotion of social change, conceived in a similar way as it was oriented from state planning (Memoirs of the first national congress of sociology) (Escalante, 1963).

After this initial meeting, two facts allow to characterize the effort made by the first professionals in sociology in the academic and research field. The first was the creation in 1964 of the Programa Latinoamericano de Estudios para el Desarrollo (Latin American Program of Development Studies)—Pledes (1965–1969), a postgraduate program that responded to the interest in developmentalist projects promoted in several countries of the continent, as to the attempt to build a common language for regional "progress" in this matter.

Like many of the initiatives that managed to materialize in this period, the Pledes of the Universidad Nacional de Colombia was able to operate, during its four years of existence, thanks to the support of international cooperators such as Ford, Fullbright, UNESCO and the universities of Wisconsin and Münster. Urban, rural and industrial transformations were the focus of interest that connected public policy, external financing and sociological work in a pioneering program of Latin American sociology. Jorge Graciarena, Luis A. Costa Pinto and Guillermo Briones, among other outstanding sociologists, passed through its classrooms, (Cataño, 1980, pp. 57–58). Its early closure is related to the strong criticism surrounding foreign financing which, in the late 1960s, began to be labeled as colonialist and imperialist intervention.

In relation to the research work, results were reflected in documents with great impact on public opinion. Texts such as *La familia en Colombia* (Family in Colombia) by Virginia Gutiérrez de Pineda (1963) were addressing problems that, just as they would become specific thematic lines (Anzola, 1990, p. 38), exposed an unused thoroughness in the analysis of social phenomena of this type. But certainly, *La violencia en Colombia* (Violence in Colombia) (Guzmán et al., 1962) placed sociology at the center of the national debate. The book, written by Orlando Fals Borda, Germán Guzmán Campos and Eduardo Umaña Luna, marked a turning point for research, as well as for the reference that would be made to the discipline over the course of several decades in the country.

As a result of an initiative by the teachers of the Faculty of Sociology headed by Fals Borda, the investigation had as an immediate precedent the report of the Comisión Nacional Investigadora de las Causas de la Violencia en el Territorio Nacional (National Commission of Inquiry into the Causes of Violence in the National Territory), created in 1958. The main objective was not only to understand the conflict that had plagued the country for more than a decade. At the same time, attempts were made to devise possible routes for the various social groups involved to stop the violent demonstrations through which social tensions were handled. As a historical record, there was hope of stopping the crimes and overcoming the trauma that a whole generation carried (Guzmán, 1991, pp. 50–51).

This was the starting point for one of the most intense and solid lines of research in Colombian sociology. The issue of violence has occupied much of the academic production in the country, a country with decades of internal armed conflict. It also meant the construction of a certain look of suspicion upon the discipline. The conclusions of the document, in particular the attribution of responsibility to traditional the political parties, the armed forces, the Catholic Church and the media, touched sensitive fibers causing discomfort in a society that was hiding under the appearance of a civilist nation.

Also, by the hand of the national congresses, sociology in the Universidad Nacional de Colombia had another important presence for the extension of the discipline in the country. Since before the publication of La violencia en Colombia, its teachers proposed the creation of a series of teaching materials between translations, monographs and research reports. These documents were cardinal in the training of professionals and in the creation of other programs in different regions because, without documentation and research centers, the environment for exchange and debate was still in its infancy.

In this way, the program of the Universidad Nacional de Colombia was the one that set the initial tone in the academic-investigative development of sociological work in the country. While the other two pioneering programs, in the Pontificia Universidad Bolivariana and the Pontificia Universidad Javeriana, for obvious reasons were guided by the social doctrine of the Church, they also reflected some of the concerns and practices of the former, in particular, the interest in the development of an applied sociology. Thus, the main point of convergence, turned out to be the arduous commitment with communities, with small groups, to be able to intervene on concrete social problems.

This is a fundamental aspect in the orientation of sociology during the early years of the 1960s. By the hand of welfare policies created by the state, charitable actions by the Church and other private organizations, and the strength that some sectors were taking in the transformations that the country suffered during this period, for these years there was still no vision of social problems as structural issues of the current social model. The diagnosis was limited to the possibilities of direct intervention in order to find immediate solutions to the difficulties experienced by specific social groups, especially those considered vulnerable.

Beyond these points of convergence, unlike the program in the Universidad Nacional de Colombia, the Javeriana and the Bolivariana did not have professionals in sociology among their promoters when it came to shaping the curricula. Its opening in these universities corresponded to an institutional directive from which it was intended to understand and act on the social world, but preserving a Christian perspective (Páez, 1996, p. 70). However, the attempt to create a field of research from sociology, led them to travel the same paths in search of suitable personnel for training and research, as well as the spaces in which professional practice could develop.

On the other hand, it is worth noting that these institutions, being private, had to overcome other obstacles related mainly to the sources of financing. Being heavily dependent on student tuition fees, the cost-effectiveness criterion sometimes worked to determine the continuity of programs. For sure, what sustained for some time the interest in sociology is closely related to what was historically configured, in these universities run by Catholic communities, as a genuine concern around "the social question".

With a long experience of community work, embodied mainly in pastoral labor, the base members of the various religious orders were closely acquainted with the difficult conditions in which the less privileged social sectors lived. Although charity was thought to be the best mechanism to alleviate poverty and inequality, the need to obtain new tools of understanding around different social problems was evident, all in the spirit of being able to act more effectively on them. Hence the interest in sociology.

Based on the social doctrine of the Church, these programs were initially aimed at training experts that promoted transformations in various areas (Arboleda, 1959, pp. 57–58). With special attention issues related to the working and peasant world were addressed, in the search to strengthen community processes advanced in their nearest environment (Ocampo, 1978, p. 128), in groups already organized by the church itself. Of course, one of the central issues, which most worried, was that of secularization, to which social tensions were attributed and which ended up being resolved violently at different levels.

For this reason, numerous research projects had to do with the loss of Christian values and its consequences in terms of social cohesion. There was also concern about the tone of workers', student and peasant demands, which were increasingly close to leftist ideas. In this way, important centers such as the Instituto de Investigaciones Socio Religiosas (Institute of Socio-religious Research), created in Colombia in 1958 as other international organizations, with professionals in sociology from Catholic universities, served as a basis for the institutionalization of higher education programs in Catholic establishments.

In the case of the Javeriana, one of the first prominent figures was Maria Cristina Salazar, who directed the department during the first years. Javerian graduate of philosophy, she had studied sociology at the Catholic University of Washington. Salazar, although relied on previous experiences of this institution, as was the Instituto de Estudios Sociales (Institute of Social Studies) created in 1957 by Vicente Andrade Valderrama S.J., soon looked at developments at the Universidad Nacional de Colombia trying to insert some changes into the initial conception of the undergraduate program at the Jesuit university. This was one of the reasons that led to her early dismissal.

While the Bolivariana program was promoted by the archdiocesan curia of Medellín, the one of the Javeriana was born in the light of an agreement with Caritas Colombia. Both contained subjects that were considered indispensable at the time, such as general sociology and some specialized, mainly urban and rural sociology, which addressed the area of methodology and techniques, as well as those with which interdisciplinary training was complemented (history, economy, geography...). All the programs also, as already indicated, advocated direct fieldwork with communities of interest.

The difference with the National University's program, was concentrated in those subjects such as labor, community, and of course, the study of encyclicals, Catholic social doctrine, dogma or family morality.[1] These differences, along with the demands that started appearing in the students about the teaching staff and their suitability to cover other sociological perspectives, especially Marxism, began to press for changes that, in the construction of new proposals, were not entirely well received by university directives.

Twist of the Nut: Extension of the Sociological Exercise at a National Level

Since the first half of the twentieth century, due to the growth of industrialization and the consequent urbanization, it had become evident the need to think of an alternative model of society that would allow overcoming certain social gaps between the inhabitants of the region, as well as the distance between this and the countries that had led the development of the capitalist system on a global level.

Consequently, under the idea of achieving "modernity" built on a developmentalist perspective as a social change oriented from above, determinant in state policy, enthusiasm was generated about the potential of sociology (Roitman, 2008, p. 36). From there it is understood the strong support given to the initiatives to create the first centers of formation and research in the area and, in particular, the influence of a current as structural functionalism, dominant by then in the schools of sociology (Moli, 2011).

---

[1] Archivo histórico Javeriana (Javeriana's Historical Archive). Rector Collection. Jesús Emilio Ramírez, S.J. 1962. Folder 17. Folio 009.

State planning instances, as well as the still incipient base of public and private social organizations, concerned about what was then read as the social question, found an important ally that lent economic and technical resources for a scientific development of practical and rapid utility, in the short and medium term. Foreign aid agencies offering such resources were mostly North American, although some Europeans were also quite active (Szymanski, 1973).

This aid had as an important framework the infrastructure created after the Second World War, in particular, that which worked for the care of the population and the reconstruction of the cities affected by the conflict. Once this purpose was advanced, resources began to be directed to the, at the time misnamed, third world. Areas of Africa and Latin America received special attention with large amounts of money and specialized personnel that was largely destined for scientific development and, among this, for the social and human sciences (Picó, 2003).

For the Latin American case this aid, which would soon be read as intervention, spread with the so-called "good-neighbourly" policies, extended in the region after the Cuban Revolution (1959). This was a milestone that marked Latin American foreign policy, as the internal development of each country in terms of national security (Gil, 2011). While most Latin American countries saw this control through the support of the United States to military regimes, in Colombia there was no need to reach this point because the northern country found in the coffee nation the best ally to maintain its area of influence.

Chile and Colombia were two of the prominent recipients of this aid, that began to be early criticized for the political implications that were read in the context of the moment. Plans as the Camelot in Chile (Navarro & Quesada, 2010), or the Simpático in Colombia, showed the porous terrain that opened up between the financing of science and its social use. And, although Colombia did not have to see military coups; what occurred was no less violent than what happened in the rest of the countries of the region because there was also repression, forced disappearance, torture and murder.

The perception created around sociology as the ideal route to understand and act on the most pressing problems has already been mentioned. Early on, it had had the support of governmental bodies so, while sociologists worked in classrooms and went out to the field to investigate, they also held public positions, some of them of high rank. This circumstance at the same time explains why sociology programs found a place in confessional universities given the Church's concern for cultural change, to which it could not respond with its traditional structures.

But this situation changed quickly. One of the breaking points would be the publication of the book La violencia en Colombia as already mentioned. Works like this, however, for the discipline, brought profound changes in a country facing new challenges. Both Fals Borda himself and what will be the commitment to Participatory Action Research (Investigación Acción Participativa)—IAP—as a way to give meaning to sociological work through social responsibility, and the political mobilization that would countenance the figure of Camilo Torres, are phenomena that express this change. This latter fact is quite significant.

Faced with the closure of new social and political forces implied by the National Front, together with the growing siege of the peasant population, even by state forces, which led to the formation of the first peasant self-defense groups, the country was shaken by a fact that, although it seemed something usual in Latin America during the Cold War, in Colombia it ended up defining the direction of the nation for the next decades (Archila, 2008, pp. 91–104).

If with the National Front the pacification of the rural world, shaken by violence, had been achieved, this system of government also promoted the organization of insurgent groups in the country. Between 1960 and 1970 the Movimiento Obrero Estudiantil y Campesino (Student and Peasant Workers' Movement)—MOEC, the Fuerzas Armadas Revolucionarias de Colombia (Revolutionary Armed Forces of Colombia)—FARC, the Ejército de Liberación Nacional (National Liberation Army)—ELN, the Ejército Popular de Liberación (Popular Liberation Army)—EPL and the Movimiento 19 de Abril (April 19 Movement)—M19—were born (Palacios, 1995, pp. 265–269). These groups were made up of people from different sectors; but it will be those members linked to the social and political sciences who carry the strongest weight of distrust from the establishment.

Thus, if on the one hand the way in which the social sciences critically analyzed the social order was beginning to be seen with some suspicion, in turn, these sciences questioned themselves in an exercise of self-reflection. The initial development of sociology, which went hand in hand with a vision of a science applied to concrete problems, of short- and medium-term resolution, led to a strong reaction, especially from the students, that ended with the reformulation of the curricula and even, at times, with the expulsion of teachers and the rejection of foreign funding.

Several facts made the crisis manifest. Confronted with the democratic closure, people like Camilo Torres Restrepo, who from very early in his priestly life had carried out important work in urban sectors, as well as in the study of violence, decided to take action through a political movement, the Frente Unido (United Front). However, faced with what he considered an insurmountable reality of democratic closure, he decided to join the Ejército de Liberación Nacional, one of the various guerrillas that were created in Colombia in the 1960s.

At the second National Sociology Congress (1967), organized under the presidency of Orlando Fals Borda, concerns for the teaching of sociology and its possibilities for institutionalization were no longer expressed. Without the presence of Torres, who was assassinated in the ranks of the ELN a year earlier, and with the increase of violence due to political and military pressure not only to the emerging insurgent groups, but mainly to the peasant population, the discussion focused on the sense of sociology and the commitment acquired from there to social transformation.

In this line, the sociology developed in the late 1950s and early 1960s in which intervention work was prioritized on vulnerable sectors was criticized. Now the issue was about the structural problems of Colombian society in which high levels of inequality and exclusion could no longer be hidden. At the same time, the neutrality of a perspective such as the developmentalist, that until now had served as a basis for thinking about social change in the region, was questioned.

Opening of New Programs

Between 1965 and 1967, five new sociology programs were opened in Colombia, two in Bogota and three in Medellin. Among these, three arose within Catholic universities, the Santo Tomás (1965), La Salle (1966) and the San Buenaventura (1967); one in a secular private university, the Autónoma Latinoamericana (1967) and the last in a public one, the Universidad de Antioquia (1968).

In the Santo Tomás, a university run by the Order of Preachers, a central precedent for the creation of the program was the work carried out by the group of Economy and Humanism at the head of Louis-Joseph Lebret O.P. Under the baton of the rector, Friar Luis J. Torres O.P., a career was devised with emphasis on technical training but with a humanist tone typical of "Christian spiritualism" (Páez et al., 2019). On the side of the San Buenaventura, its origin was in the Institute of Socio-family Sciences from where the creation an academic space for sociology was proposed, by the Archdiocese of Medellin, with the priest Friar Arturo Calle at the head.

Other non-confessional training centers such as the Universidad Autónoma Latinoamericana, created to defend the principles of academic freedom and university autonomy, had intellectuals like Luis Antonio Restrepo and Álvaro Tirado Mejía guiding a program focused on social research. Due to the character of the university, they also bet on the study of Latin America and, from sociology, on one that supported social transformation (Robledo & Beltrán, 2005). At the Universidad de Antioquia, a public and secular institution, Saturnino Sepulveda was the priest who drew attention to the need to train professionals to address the rapid social changes in the country and, in particular, for the regional situation, to the accelerated process of industrialization.

The way in which these new programs were conceived replicated the curriculum that was considered usual for the teaching of sociology. Three fundamental areas formed the nucleus: sociological theories (classical and, what at the time was classified as, contemporary); methodologies and techniques, and so-called special sociologies. According to the character of the institution, different emphasis was placed on the subjects that functioned for an interdisciplinary formation, whether they were part of the social sciences or of philosophy, economics and political science.

One of the expressions that allowed to give a particular profile to each program was the concentration on specific special sociologies, including rural, urban, labor, or industrial sociology, just to mention a few. Among the denominational universities, the interest to understand and act on the family, education and community development was highlighted. The Universidad de Antioquia, on the other bank, stood out for deepening Marxism and accompanying processes of strengthening social movements (Serna, 1996, pp. 148–149).

Except for the latter, the newly opened programs were running for about a decade, closed shortly afterwards, mostly because of the low enrollment. Those who were most interested in the community sector, ultimately, saw sociology as a craft for small and medium-scale social intervention, aimed at transforming the environment of the most vulnerable groups, set up their training plans in night schools. With the latter, the number of students in the Universidad Autónoma Latinoamericana was important, although the Universidad Pontificia Bolivariana also had this modality at a time of boom in the discipline during the 1970s.

The progressive closing of programs came hand in hand with a competition that proved to better clarify a professional profile from the area of economics and political science, profiles that dominated the labor field that at another time had been thought for sociologists. At the same time, the closeness between sociological research and the possibilities of social impact through the formulation and development of public policies, was extinguished with the erosion, and strong criticism, of the developmentalist perspectives that pointed towards the "modernization".

However, other attempts to promote sociology at the regional level led to the creation of new programs. In the Colombian Caribbean, the Universidad Autónoma del Caribe (1969) and the Universidad Simón Bolívar (1972) (Bolívar, 2021) promoted higher education, although their programs did not consolidate a research and teaching team (González, 1996, p. 196) reason why they closed in the 1980s (Beltrán & Orozco, 2021, p. 107). However, these were important centers for the formation of a new generation that opened the debate around the dominant issues in the country and put others on the table, such as those related to the cultural field.

In the east of the country, in the city of Bucaramanga, the Universidad Cooperativa de Colombia created the sociology program in 1976 as an extension of one created a year earlier in Bogota. Due to the institutional mission of the university, the relationship between sociology and cooperativism was the axis of formation and social intervention. Most of their students were workers who attended classes at night. In the west, the Universidad del Valle became the third public university in the country to open its classrooms to sociology.

Univalle program began operating in 1978, quickly becoming one of the most prominent. The effort advanced by the group of teachers, who gave particular importance to the training of researchers (Valencia, 2019, p. 60), illustrates the debates that at the end of the 1960s and the beginning of the 1970s led to the reformulation of the sociology programs that existed at that time and which, precisely, guided the creation of the latter (Hernández, 1996).

The focus of these debates was the Universidad Nacional de Colombia, from which the reform of the curriculum was advanced. There, the defense was initiated for the development of a politically committed sociology, in view of the active transformation of Colombian society. Thus, in a process led by teachers, a total renewal of the training program was made in 1968, a decade after its entry into operation (Restrepo, 2002, pp. 185–186).

This reform triggered others in the various sociology programs in the country and was the basis for the creation of new ones.

The strongest criticism was directed towards what was read as the instrumental view of sociology. The close relationship between the work of researchers and the demands of private organizations and state bodies was considered a subordination of the scientific function to partial interests. Attention was also drawn to the minimal impact of the work carried out so far, since at best some palliative measures had been considered that did not resolve the conditions of insecurity of large sectors of the population. Structural functionalism yielded to Marxism, while in the region movement occurred from the developmentalist perspective to the theory of dependence.

The growth of a committed sociology was fueled in the country by shocking events. The main one was perhaps the death of Camilo Torres Restrepo, in 1966, in his first combat in the ranks of the ELN. The decision to fight in the mountains to seek for what had not been achieved in the city, foreshadowed an idea about the scope of the discipline itself. Fals Borda, in turn, left the sociology department and the Universidad Nacional de Colombia. As a manager of important resources, he was target of provident criticism from those who saw in international financing a mechanism of imperialist interference.

On the other hand, among the religious communities that created sociology programs in Catholic universities, other events such as the Second Vatican Council (1962–1965) or the Conference of Medellin (1968) nourished this same idea. Without denying the strong internal tensions between the ecclesiastical hierarchy and the bases, the option for the poor intensified the practice of a committed sociology that on many occasions led to militancy shoulder to shoulder with peasant and workers sectors. In Colombia the clearest example was the Golconda group; in Latin America, the Liberation Theology.

Reorientation of Sociology at the National Level

As already mentioned, both the social crisis stemming from the system of restricted democracy of the National Front governments, as the criticism of the sociological model that closely followed the developmentalist perspective of social change, led to a profound transformation in the conception of discipline until then. That training of functional professionals to the idea of planning from above, aligned with the state and private proposals of intervention in the communities (Guzmán, 1983, pp. 112–115), was revalued under the prism of what it meant to transfigure the current social system.

The call was made for the construction of an owned science. Amid the tensions of the Cold War, external financing became the first target of attacks, especially North American, financing that had certainly been central to the development of sociology in the country (García, 2013). This demand was articulated with others that were gaining strength within the student movement, from the promotion of academic freedom and decision-making on central research issues, to the condemnation of violence and the constant repression suffered by the social mobilization (Robledo & Beltrán, 2008).

The impact of the student movement was felt in the closure of some sociology programs; the case of the Javeriana is, perhaps, the one that had greatest notoriety. In this university, students and professors met in the Movimiento Cataluña (Catalonia Movement) whose demands and forms of protest generated the reaction of the directives leading to the closure of the career (Galeano, 2012) for more than 30 years. In the 1970s, a total of eight sociology programs were discontinued at the higher level, mostly in private universities ran by religious communities.

Hand in hand with student demands related to the updating of curricula, participation in university government and training that responded to the problems of the country, limited funding provided the basis for the closure of departments. The resources available to these private institutions came mostly from tuition fees, with exclusive support through teaching, which is why the decrease in students directly affected the operation of the programs.

This crisis was compounded by the temporary closure of the programs of the Universidad Nacional de Colombia and the University de Antioquia along with the dismantling of the Asociación Colombiana de Sociología. The Association at that time, as still today, brought together mostly people who were professionally linked to the academy, marginalizing other groups that have worked in organizations of various types or in non-institutional investigations. Beyond this difficulty, it has also served as a basis for the extension of sociology at the regional level.

These transformations on a different scale in sociological training and practice are part of important political reforms that took place in the country. The end of the National Front was sought in the middle of the decade.

The opening to the democratic game occurred at a time when the numerous insurgent groups were growing and strengthening, as civil society channeled their disagreements through a strong presence in the streets, as expressed by the 1977 civic strike. This new balance of forces led to strong responses from the elites such as the establishment of the Estatuto de Seguridad (Security Statute).

In this manner, while in Colombia the consetionalist pact ended, in the rest of Latin America one of the darkest periods began. In several countries of the region, dictatorships were imposed under the consent of the elites while the United States good-neighborly policy was disappearing in terms of the different aids that had fed the development of the social sciences in this part of the hemisphere. Colombia, without a dictatorship, also responded to the criminalization of the left through the configuration of the "internal enemy".

By the end of the 1970s and the beginning of the next decade, the country was plunged into a new spiral of violence in which, along with the strengthening of the armed insurgency, armed right-wing groups appeared to justify their actions under the idea of containing this internal enemy. The deterioration of the armed conflict would be accompanied by the rise and spread of drug trafficking, a phenomenon that even today is one of the most complex and problematic when it comes to finding solutions to this conflict. At the end of this period, sociology oscillated, in the eyes of the outside, as a promoter of subversive movements or as a science supporting imperialist politics.

Research Opening and Central Themes of Colombian Sociology at the End of the Twentieth Century

In the 1980s there is an important presence of sociologists working in state institutions again, both in planning offices in support of social programs, as well as in universities. This is also the decade in which work with NGOs would open a new workplace (Restrepo & Restrepo, 1997, pp. 17–18) due, especially, to the opportunities provided by the government of Belisario Betancur (1982–1986) and peace negotiations with insurgent groups. Outside the institutions, social and political movements were supported (Londoño, 1980, p. 104). However, with the large number of graduates, new difficulties arose in finding employment (Anzola, 1990, p. 59).

In this period, with a new reactivation of the Asociación Colombiana de Sociología, other conferences were scheduled at level: *Sociología, balances y perspectivas* (Sociology, balances and perspectives) (Bogotá, 1980); *La investigación sociológica hoy* (Sociological research today) (Medellín 1982), *Poder político y estructura social* (Political power and social structure) (Medellín, 1985); *Dinámica social y cultura regional* (Social dynamics and regional culture) (Bucaramanga 1987) and *Violencia, cultura y cambio social* (Violence, culture and social change) (Barranquilla, 1989). The names in part are indicative of the central discussions that went through the sociological exercise during this period.

The research that stood out during these years has a greater thematic breadth, a breadth that is related in part to the strengthening of programs and centers that managed to hold in several cities in the country (Vega, 2021, p. 10). In this direction, regional studies can be mentioned around questions about migration and colonization, questions that joined inquiries in the area of rural conflicts. Books such as Historia doble de la Costa written by Fals Borda (1979–1984), or the texts of Alfredo Molano and his exhibition on social conflicts in different places, through social biographies, marked an important course in this field (Camacho & Hernández, 1990).

Among other sociologists who were interested in such studies, close to rural conflicts, are Jaime Eduardo Jaramillo (1988), Fernando Cubides et al. (1986), Maria Teresa Findji and Rojas (1985); or its more direct relationship with the problem of drug trafficking with the work of Álvaro Camacho Guizado (1981). This thematic nucleus continued to be closely related to investigations into violence, on which a number of investigations have been conducted (Molano & Reyes, 1980; Ortíz, 1985).

Gender issues began to have a greater presence during these years with the analysis of the educational, labor and political situation of women and, in particular, the levels of inequity and inequality, as well as increased attention to maternity (Bonilla, 1983, p. 303). However, the discussions were closer to family issues than to feminism, being a concern that entered the research agenda mainly of women, among them Elsy Bonilla (1985), Magdalena León (1977), Nohra Segura (1990), Ana Rico (1986), Rafaela Vos Obeso, just to mentioned a few.

By the late 1980s, the national congress in Barranquilla was the scene of debate on a certain hierarchy of research topics and issues that had been established in Colombia. During the preparatory stages of the event, many asked to direct the gaze towards sociology of culture, especially because in the Colombian Caribbean there was already an important trajectory in the analysis of popular festivals and carnivals (Rey, 1987, p. 241) with authors such as Hernando Parra, Blas de Zubiría and Rey Sinning (Correa, 2016, pp. 202–210).

For the rest, other specialized sociologies were strengthened with studies around the sociology and history of science (Obregón, 1991; Restrepo, 1985), of education (Parra, 1986), of industry, technology, labor (Mayor, 1984, Weiss, 1994, Rainer Dombois, 1990, Urrea, 1976) and of unionism (Londoño et al., 1986).

Names mentioned here only illustrate certain problems of interest, far from accounting for all production in the field of the discipline. Their allusion is a way of exemplifying the various topics in which Colombian sociology developed until the 1990s. This agenda, which drew attention for trying to overcome the predominant themes and issues during the opening of the first programs, particularly those related to social conflict and violence, had to turn the look once more at them.

This period was again characterized by a highly violent moment, especially against social movements and leftist parties. The spread of drug trafficking, with the generation of an unprecedented amount of economic resources in the country, ended up financing various armed sectors at a time when peace processes with insurgent groups had not yet been consolidated. The proceeds of illicit drug trafficking served to strengthen existing groups as well as to create new ones, mostly parastatals, that advanced countless death and displacement actions.

The 1980s closed with a peace process with the M-19 guerrilla while the 1990s opened with a new political constitution. In the meantime, a dirty war led to the extermination of a political party, the Unión Patriótica (Patriotic Union) (Archila, 2008, pp. 116–119). For sociology, during those years the program of the Universidad Santo Tomás was reopened and others were created at the Universidad del Atlántico (1999) and the Universidad Popular del Cesar (2000) (Angulo & Nieves, 2021, pp. 170–172), as well as at the Universidad del Rosario. In 2005, the program of the Pontificia Universidad Javeriana was reopened.

At the same time, some research centers were created that allowed the development of a more interdisciplinary work positioning social sciences; among them, the Instituto de Estudios Políticos y Relaciones Internacionales (Institute of Political Studies and International Relations)—IEPRI and the Centro de Estudios Sociales (Center for Social Studies)—CES at the Universidad Nacional de Colombia, as well as the

Centro de Investigación y Documentación Socioeconómica (Center for Socioeconomic Research and Documentation) at the Universidad del Valle. Sociologists also found space at the Centro de Investigación y Acción Popular (Center for Popular Research and Action)—Cinep and at Foro Nacional por Colombia (National Forum for Colombia), among other centers.

Thus closed the twentieth century. In 40 years the development of an applied, empirical sociology with the aim of training expert researchers to support the planning projects directed mostly by the national government, was surpassed by a critical sociology that challenged the perspective that defended "development", given the structural problems of Colombia and the region.

A body of study was formed with different lines of inquiry, oriented to the problems that were considered most relevant, both in historical vision and also in conjunctural situations. Unfortunately, in the middle of the various violent demonstrations throughout the national territory, the issue of armed conflict became one of the central topics when consolidating the research field of sociology in Colombia. Even so, the growing professional body, in various places of the academic and research exercise, has allowed an amplitude of views that enhance the sociological knowledge in various areas, areas that continue to enrich and qualify in contemporary work.

REFERENCES

Angulo, F., & Nieves, R. (2021). La sociología. Una nueva praxis en el departamento del cesar. In J. Vega y H. Parra (Dir.), *50 años de la sociología académica en el Caribe Colombiano* (pp. 165–178). Ed. Uninorte.

Anzola, B. (1990). *Desarrollo de la sociología en Colombia. Décadas 60 y 70. Trabajo de pregrado sociología.* Universidad de la Salle.

Arboleda, J. (1959). *Las ciencias sociales en Colombia.* Centro Latinoamericano de Investigaciones en Ciencias Sociales.

Archila, M. (2008). *Idas y venidas. Vueltas y revueltas. Protestas sociales en Colombia 1958–1990.* Icanh, Cinep.

Beltrán, C., & Orozco, M. (2021). La sociología en la Universidad Autónoma del Caribe. In J. Vega y H. Parra (Dir.), *50 años de la sociología académica en el Caribe Colombiano* (pp. 89–110). Ed. Uninorte.

Bolívar, J. (2021). La sociología en la Universidad Simón Bolívar. In J. Vega y H. Parra (dir.), *50 años de la sociología académica en el Caribe Colombiano* (pp. 111–134). Ed. Uninorte.

Bonilla, E. (1983). La investigación sobre la mujer: logros y perspectivas In *La sociedad colombiana y la investigación sociológica* (pp. 303–312). Guadalupe.

Bonilla, E. (1985). *Mujer y familia en Colombia*. Plaza & Janés Ed.

Camacho, A. (1981). *Droga, corrupción y poder: marihuana y cocaína en la sociedad colombiana*. Univalle.

Camacho, A., & Hernández, J. (1990). *Qué sabemos, qué no sabemos y por qué: un intento de evaluación de la investigación sociológica en Colombia en la década de los ochenta*. Cidse.

Cataño, G. (1980). La sociología en Colombia: un balance. In *La sociología en Colombia. Balance y perspectivas* (pp. 51–81). Bogotá. Colciencias.

Correa, A. (2016). *Sociología desde el caribe colombiano. Mirada de un sentipensante* (J. Vega (Comp.). Universidad del Norte.

Cubides, F., Jaramillo, J., & Mora, L. (1986). *Colonización, coca y guerrilla*. UN.

Dombois, R. (1990). *Organización empresarial y formación de obreros en la industria: un estudio de caso sobre una empresa del sector automotriz colombiano*. UN.

Findji, M., & Rojas, M. (1985). *Territorio, economía y sociedad*. Univalle.

Galeano, J. (2012). *La historia de un movimiento. Movimiento Estudiantil Javeriano (1968–1972)*. Tesis pregrado en Historia. PUJ.

García, M. (2013). Universidad Pública Colombiana y fundaciones norteamericanas en el contexto de las reformas universitarias, 1960-1966: los casos de la Universidad del Valle y de la Universidad Nacional de Colombia. *Anuario de Historia Regional y de las Fronteras, 18*(2), 439–469. https://revistas.uis.edu.co/index.php/anuariohistoria/article/view/3878

Gil, G. (2011). Ciencias Sociales, Imperialismo y Filantropía. Dilemas y Conflictos en torno a la Fundación Ford en la Argentina de los '60. *Revista Argentina de Sociología, 8-9*, 153–181. https://www.redalyc.org/articulo.oa?id=26922386008

González, A. (1996). La sociología académica en Barranquilla: un segundo aliento. In *La sociología en Colombia. Estado académico* (pp. 187–208). Icfes.

Gutiérrez, V. (1963). *La familia en Colombia. Trasfondo histórico*. Fac Sociología UN.

Guzmán, A. (1983). La acción comunal y los pobladores de Cali. In *La sociedad colombiana y la investigación sociológica* (pp. 111–130). Bogotá.

Guzmán, G. (1991). Reflexión crítica sobre el libro "La violencia en Colombia". In G. Sánchez y R. Peñaranda (Comp.), *Pasado y presente de la violencia en Colombia* (pp. 45–60). Cerec.

Guzmán, G., Fals, B. O., & Umaña, E. (1962). *La violencia en Colombia*. UN.

Hernández, J. (1996). Hacer sociología en Colombia: el primer cuarto de siglo en la experiencia de una comunidad académica. In *La sociología en Colombia. Estado académico* (pp. 69–110). Icfes.

Jaramillo, J. (1988). *Estado, sociedad y campesinos*. Tercer Mundo Ed.

Jaramillo, J. (2020). Los orígenes de la sociología profesional en Colombia: Camilo Torres, proyección académica, investigación científica y actividad social y política (1959–1964). S. Vanegas (Coord.). In *Trayectorias y proyectos intelectuales. El pensamiento social en América Latina y Colombia* (pp. 104–128). PUJ.

León, M. (1977). *La mujer y el desarrollo en Colombia*. Asociación colombiana para el estudio de la población.

Londoño, R. (1980). Una experiencia de la investigación marxista en Colombia. In *La sociología en Colombia. Balance y perspectivas* (pp. 103–130). Bogotá. Colciencias.

Londoño, R., Gómez, H., & Perry, G. (1986). In M. Cárdenas (Ed.), *Sindicalismo y política económica*. Fedesarrollo-CEREC.

Mayor, A. (1984). *Ética, trabajo y productividad en Antioquia: una interpretación sociológica sobre la influencia de la Escuela Nacional de Minas en la vida, costumbres e industrialización regionales*. Tercer mundo Ed.

Molano, A., & Reyes, A. (1980). *Los bombardeos en el Pato*. Cinep.

Moli, E. (2011). La institucionalización de la sociología en América latina. Ruptura y culminación encarnados en los casos de Gino Germani y Florestán Fernandes. *IX Jornadas de Sociología. Facultad de Ciencias Sociales, Universidad de Buenos Aires* (pp. 1–16). https://cdsa.aacademica.org/000-034/596.pdf

Navarro, J., & Quesada, F. (2010). El impacto del proyecto Camelot en el período de consolidación de las ciencias sociales latinoamericanas. In D. Pereyra (Comp.), *El desarrollo de las ciencias sociales. Tradiciones, actores e instituciones en Argentina, Chile, México y Centroamérica*. Cuaderno de ciencias sociales 153. Flacso.

Obregón, D. (1991). *Surgimiento de las sociedades científicas en Colombia 1859–1936*. Tesis posgrado en Historia. UN.

Ocampo, C. (1978). 20 años de la Facultad de Sociología UPB. Fundación y evolución de su currículo. *Revista de sociología, 9*(13), 126–132.

Ortíz, C. (1985). *Estado y subversión en Colombia: la violencia en el Quindío, años 50*. Cerec.

Páez, G. (1996). Estado del arte de los programas de Sociología en las universidades privadas de Santa Fe de Bogotá. In *La sociología en Colombia. Estado académico* (pp. 69–110). Icfes.

Páez, G., Clavijo, G., Narváez, G. E., Salazar, V., & y Urra, M. (2019). Aportes de la Universidad Santo Tomás a la institucionalización de la sociología en Colombia en los años sesenta y setenta. *Campos en Ciencias Sociales, 7*(1), 227–247. https://doi.org/10.15332/25006681.4549

Palacios, M. (1995). *Entre la legitimidad y la violencia. Colombia 1875–1994*. Norma.

Parra, R. (1975). *El surgimiento de una comunidad científica en un país subdesarrollado. La sociología en Colombia 1959–1969*. S.n.

Parra, R. (1986). *Los maestros colombianos*. Plaza & Janés.

Picó, J. (2003). *Los años dorados de la sociología (1945–1975)*. Alianza Ed.

Restrepo, G. (2002). *Peregrinación en pos de omega: sociología y sociedad en Colombia*. UN.

Restrepo, G., & Restrepo, O. (1997). Balance doble de treinta años de historia. In *La sociología en Colombia. Estado académico* (pp. 3–67). Icfes.

Restrepo, O. (1985). Perspectivas de la historia y la sociología de las ciencias. In *Colombia, ciencia tecnología y desarrollo*. Colciencias.

Rey, E. (1987). Capital y carnaval. In *V Congreso Nacional de sociología. Poder político y estructura social en Colombia*. Bogotá, Icfes. Ed. Guadalupe.

Rico, A. (1986). *Madres solteras adolescentes*. Plaza & Janés.

Robledo, L., & Beltrán, M. (2005). Los "Años Dorados" de la Sociología en Medellín (1967–1971). *Sociología: Revista De La Facultad De Sociología De Unaula, 28*, 31–45.

Robledo, L., & Beltrán, M. (2008). *La sociología desde la universidad: luces y sombras de los programas académicos en Medellín. 1978–1998*. Informe de investigación inédito. Universidad de Antioquia.

Roitman, M. (2008). *Pensar América Latina. El desarrollo de la sociología latinoamericana*. Clacso.

Segura, N. (1990). *Mujer y sociedad: estudios, balances y perspectivas*. Univalle.

Serna, A. (1996). Una mirada a la sociología en Medellín. In *La sociología en Colombia. Estado académico* (pp. 145–183). Icfes.

Szymanski, A. (1973). Las fundaciones internacionales y América Latina. *Revista mexicana de sociología, 35*(4), 801–817. https://www.jstor.org/stable/i282378

Urrea, F. (1976). *Mercados de trabajo y migraciones en la explotación cafetera*. Senalde.

Valencia, A. (2019). Sociología en provincia. Los programas de la Universidad del Valle (Cali, Colombia). *Revista Colombiana de. Sociología, 42*(2), 47–66. https://doi.org/10.15446/rcs.v42n2.57867

Vega, J. (2021). Apuntes a mano alzada sobre los cincuenta años de la sociología académica en el caribe colombiano. In J. Vega & H. Parra (Dir.), 50 años de la sociología académica en el Caribe Colombiano (pp. 9–34). Ed. Uninorte.

Vergara, F. (1997). *Ciento catorce años de la sociología en Colombia*. Sistemas y Computadores Ltda.

Weiss, A. (1994). *La empresa colombiana entre la tecnocracia y la participación: del taylorismo a la calidad total*. Bogotá.

Escalante, C. (1963). Convocatoria. In *Memorias del primer congreso nacional de sociología*. Bogotá. Iqueima.

CHAPTER 4

Church, State and Academia

Abstract This chapter focuses on the relationship between Catholic networks of international cooperation and the processes of academic institutionalization of sociology in Colombia. This has been a topic little explored when telling the history of the discipline in the country and in the region. However, the weight of the Catholic Church as an institution, at the time of the creation of the first university programs of sociology in the mid-twentieth century, cannot go unnoticed.

Despite the early and crucial support coming from this source, it was fractured by external and internal reasons of the church itself. Among the first, the changes that led to the configuration of a critical and committed sociology. Among the latter, the new path that opened since the Second Vatican Council. Still, the "option for the poor" characterized the close correspondence between Christian thought and social sciences since the mid-1960s. For the case of sociology in Colombia, Camilo Torres Restrepo may represent the most illustrative trajectory of this process.

Keywords Sociology • Catholic Church • International cooperation • Social question

© The Author(s), under exclusive license to Springer Nature Switzerland AG 2023
J. Aldana Cedeño, *Sociology in Colombia*, Sociology Transformed,
https://doi.org/10.1007/978-3-031-39412-6_4

49

The interest aroused by sociology, expressed in the opening of training and research centers in the area, has already been addressed in the preceding chapters in relation to the reformist initiatives widespread in Colombia and in Latin America in the mid-twentieth century. Besides this interest, at the international level there was already an institutional apparatus on which the discipline had spread globally, especially that developed in the United States and in Europe. Contact with this academic community laid the foundations for the expansion of sociology in several countries of the region.

When going through different national histories in the subcontinent, with emphasis on its academic institutionalization, we usually refer to the same supports on which the spaces of sociological work were established. Although there are small temporary differences, it is argued that the impetus given by university directives, hand in hand with work with government entities, was crucial in securing the initial resources for the creation of the first training programs at higher level.

In addition to these sectors, in Latin America there were several multilateral organizations that provided the framework in which the legitimacy of the knowledge generated in the field of social sciences was sustained. Some of them were the Comisión Económica para América Latina (Economic Commission for Latin America)—CEPAL (1947), and within it the Instituto Latinoamericano de Planificación Económica y Social (Latin American Institute of Economic and Social Planning)—Ilpes (1962), or the Facultad Latinoamericana de Ciencias Sociales (Latin American Faculty of Social Sciences)—Flacso (1957) (Roitman, 2008, p. 34). In turn, some philanthropic organizations, mostly North American, such the Ford, Carnegie, Rockefeller and Fullbright foundations, provided significant resources for infrastructure, training and research.

However, the Catholic Church, one of the strongest institutions in the region for centuries, at least until the middle of the twentieth century, became another support for the institutionalization of sociology in the country. With an important control of the educational system, a long-standing experience working with communities and an interest in defending certain cultural patterns that governed the majority of the population, this institution saw in sociology a possibility of reaching a more appropriate knowledge in view of its interest in social intervention.

The previous chapters have studied the work carried out by some religious communities when opening training and research programs in the area. Beyond the particular cases already mentioned, the aim is to delve here into the investigation of the role of Catholic networks of cooperation at an international level which, although central, have gone unnoticed in much of the historical narratives around the institutionalization of sociology in Latin America, except in the Chilean case.

ACTION OF THE CATHOLIC CHURCH AND THE SOCIAL QUESTION

The emergence of two of the first three university programs of professional training in sociology in Colombia, promoted by Catholic institutions, moves part of the exploration of the emergence of academic sociology towards the foundations of the Social Action of the Church which, in the country, as in some areas of Latin America, had been carrying out several decades of social work, mainly through pastoral work.

As Beigel (2011) mentions, Liberation Theology is best known in the region given the close relationship between the Church and different groups that sought a deep transformation in the social structure. However, the interest of the Catholic Church to counteract what from the nineteenth century began to be seen as the mismatches brought about by capitalist development and the extension of the liberal vision, led to undertake several programs to support, in different ways, the sectors most affected by these imbalances.

The Acción Social Católica (Catholic Social Action)—ASC—was fundamentally based on the defense of Christianity and Catholic morality, from an institution that viewed with concern the advance of liberalism and communism. In Latin America, as in much of the so-called "third world", the economic, political, social and cultural changes that accelerated since the end of the nineteenth century, and that ended with the increase of exclusion, marginality and inequality, forced the eyes of the Church on the working class, the peasantry, children and women.

During the interwar period, Pius XI, the "Pope of Catholic Action", conceived this project with the purpose of reintroducing Christian morality in society. The economic crisis of the 1930s, the way taken by capitalism and the strength of the labor movement with its orientation to the left, strengthened the postulates of the Rerum Novarum Encyclical of Leo XIII aimed at addressing the social question: the scope of the fair and family wage, the unionist organization and the real participation of the workers in industries, confronting the new forms of Marxist socialism (Escudero, 1997, pp. 80–93).

The ASC functioned through the hierarchical organization proper to the Church and, in principle, tried to maintain an apolitical character, which would later separate it from the Christian democracy (Montero, 2005, p. 135). The believers who promoted it worried about the living conditions of the marginalized population, while opposing liberalism for its anticlericalism and communism for its materialistic atheism (Bidegain, 1985, p. 20). However, the latter became the opponent to defeat in the new times.

This is the reason why no criticism of the forms of exploitation of the capitalist system was formed from there; although hard work was done to alleviate the difficult situation of the workers through mutual aid and accompaniment societies. This direction is what characterizes the development of the ASC in Colombia, a country in which historically there has been closeness between the Catholic Church and the State, proximity whose maximum expression is found in the transit of the nineteenth to the twentieth century during the Regeneración (Regeneration).[1]

Since the beginning of the twentieth century, the Colombian Catholic Church had already promoted several associations of support among workers, within the framework of the "social question" thought from the perspective of the Social Doctrine of the Church, far from any proposal of modern unionism (Archila, 1991, pp. 45–46). In the country, the Jesuits were at the head of some initiatives, in fact, Jesús María Fernández S.J. wrote in 1915 an official text with the proposal of the ASC, Manual de sociología práctica de la Acción Social Católica (Manual of practical sociology of the Catholic Social Action). In which, the need to go beyond charity and to strive better to overcome poverty was exposed.

This work had the full support of the national government as it became a first-hand mechanism to contain the rise of leftist movements, which began to swell their ranks during this period. The attention given to

---

[1] In the relationship that Cortes presents between the *Regeneración* and the Romanization-ultramontanism, the clearest example is the 1887 Concordat: "This Concordat allowed the establishment in Colombia of the Christian Regime, where the State facilitated the work of the ecclesiastical institution, and even bequeathed to it functions that directly belonged to it, such as the supervision of public education, the population control, the control of the civil status of individuals, mediated by baptismal certificates, which fulfilled the function of civil registration, and parish books, indicating the direct relationship between nationality and religion, etc." (Cortés, 1997, p. 5).

peasants and workers was advanced through charitable centers, study associations and spaces for sports practices (Bidegain, 1985, pp. 55–75), also responding to the deep concern about the secularization process that these groups were following. For this, the extensive network of parishes in neighborhoods, sidewalks and towns was used.

The Acción Católica Colombiana (Colombian Catholic Action)—ACC—was officially organized in 1933. From there, the creation of workers' and peasants' unions was encouraged while anti-communist leagues were promoted. On the other hand, in Catholic universities such as the Pontificia Universidad Bolivariana and the Pontificia Universidad Javeriana, courses on social organization were opened based on the social doctrine of the church. In 1959, the first training programs in sociology were created in these two universities, along with that of the Universidad Nacional de Colombia.

For an initial view of the role of sociology in Catholic universities, it is relevant to keep in mind that in these institutions the so-called social question, genuine concern, presented as the only way out of the social conflict, a call to Christian charity in the search for social harmony. The problem was not of the system itself, which is why there was no criticism of capitalism while liberalism became tolerable. The problem laid in the moral bases of human action; whereby human beings lost the north of salvation in heaven to concentrate on the earthly conflicts that fed violence (Beltrán, 2018, p. 111).

One of the areas of work that was relatively successful were the Catholic unions. During the Liberal Republic (1930–1946), State intervention to resolve labor conflicts proved to be effective primarily for the workers' organization itself. In 1935 the Confederación Sindical de Colombia (Union Confederation of Colombia) was created, then CTC for Confederación de Trabajadores de Colombia (Workers' Confederation of Colombia), in which the communist and liberal tendency predominated. Faced with these initiatives, the business community began to support the Church in the creation of Catholic organizations and unions throughout the national territory.

By 1939 the ACC had already established 73 unions (Plata, 2013, p. 31). In this way the Unión de Trabajadores de Antioquia (Union of Workers of Antioquia)—UTRAN—was created in 1945, as well as the Federación Nacional de Agricultores (National Federation of Farmers)—FANAL. A year later, the Unión de Trabajadores de Colombia (Union of Workers of Colombia)—UTC—appeared (Archila, 2008, pp. 360–361).

Guided in appearance by apolitical and anti-party principles, these organizations had as their central objective to raise the moral level of these sectors. Sometimes, however, they promoted the occupation of idle lands or employed strikes as a mechanism of pressure.

Beyond the criticisms that may arise from this orientation, with its inability to make a real diagnosis of the social changes that the country was going through and, to this extent, of the low probability of resolving the conflicts that it sought to avoid, these palliative actions confronted to some extent the poverty conditions of large groups of the population. In a country with an incipient capitalist development, and with an enormous social inequality, this pastoral work provided part of the basis that generated interest in sociology from confessional institutions of higher education. However, this base had a fundamental ally during the same period: Catholic transnational networks.

CATHOLIC NETWORKS FOR INTERNATIONAL COOPERATION

The social question became one of the axes of the Church's action. The Rerum Novarum encyclical focused its attention on the problems that arose due to the social, political, cultural, and economic consequences of the accelerated process of industrialization and urbanization. In response, a provision of support was configured through unions, cooperatives, and other organizations, along with the creation of study, research and dissemination centers around social problems (Arias, 2003, p. 191).

Another strategy was the foundation of Christian Democratic parties. Although in Colombia this initiative had little resonance with an attempt at organization in 1959, there was the Movimiento Social Demócrata Cristiano (Christian Social Democratic Movement), founded that same year by graduates of the Pontificia Universidad Javeriana; while the Partido Social Cristiano (Social Christian Party) had the participation of important researchers in the area of social sciences such as Virginia Gutiérrez de Pineda and María Cristina Salazar, the latter also leader of the Movimiento Cruzada Social (Social Crusade Movement) (Cifuentes, 2010, p. 34). However, the structure of the National Front led many of these leaders to migrate back to traditional parties or link up with new alternatives, including the Frente Unido (United Front).

But it was the global Catholic networks that played a central role in this regard. Through them, concern for the social question found an investigative channel in the promotion of the social sciences. Sociology, in particular, benefited from this international cooperation when undertaking its academic institutionalization in the region. This cooperation, which began as part of the aid for the reconstruction of some European countries after the Second World War, was soon transformed into a kind of "technical assistance" network, with emphasis on what were considered problems of underdevelopment.

The "underdevelopment" in Latin America not only drew attention to the evident growth of inequality, with the exclusion and marginalization of broad sectors of the population. The central political concern during this period was the possibility of the expansion of communism in the face of the progressive discontent of these same sectors. The various social problems present, their diagnosis and possible solution, motivated the unusual development of the social sciences. A number of public and private organizations began to provide funding for local research, as well as for training experts in European and North American universities.

International cooperation promoted by Catholic networks in this area began to play a prominent role since the 1940s. In addition to pastoral work in parishes and the creation of various workers' organizations, an extensive international network of Catholic organizations provided important support for the promotion of the technical and scientific development of the social sciences (Navarro, 2013).

In understanding the scope of this network, several factors need to be considered. To begin with, the Catholic Church had a long experience in the international arena thanks to its presence in different territories with the questioned missions of evangelization. Well into the twentieth century, these became humanitarian aid programs through transnational projects. As a religious group, it has also been the only institution of this type recognized as a "quasi-state", with a huge influence on other types of institutions, non-confessional, also of humanitarian aid, because of its proximity to the population and its ability to manage resources.

Among the most influential organizations in the region are the Catholic Relief Services (1943) founded by American Bishops or the Kirche in Not which was born in 1947 in Belgium. By 1951 the statutes of Caritas Internationalis had been established and it was officially named in 1954, bringing together Canadian, North American and European initiatives, which quickly spread to the rest of the world with a greater presence after the Second Vatican Council.

In 1966 the Catholic bishops of Canada founded Development and Peace; and many other organizations began work in the 1970s and 1980s.

Among the initiatives that funded numerous research programs are some from German Catholic communities, such as Misereor, created in 1958 to fight poverty in the third world, and Adveniat, founded three years later and oriented to meet the needs of Latin America and the Caribbean (Arriaga, 2013).

This development concurred with the professionalization of priests of the Catholic Church during the same period. Various Catholic experts participated in social programs in the region, in the area of social research and intervention, while student mobility was promoted to universities in different areas of knowledge, especially Leuven, Georgetown and Notre Dame. For the case of the social sciences and the tone that the institution-alization of studies in this field will take, it is also necessary to relate how in the Catholic world the "option for the poor" was gaining strength; guidance that responded to these joint efforts to address the growing problems of the global world.

As dominant organization in the political, social and cultural sphere from the Colony until well into the second half of the twentieth century, the Catholic Church played a decisive role in the region. Among the communities with the greatest presence and with a clear hegemony at an educational level, the Society of Jesus stands out, despite having been expelled three times from Colombia (in 1767, 1850 and 1861). In addition to the educational system, the "international aid" derived from other projects that served to expand and strengthen social sciences in Catholic universities.

One of these projects came from the Instrucción del apostolado social (Instruction of the Social Apostolate) published in 1949 by Jean Baptiste Janssens, Superior General of the Jesuits. It made an open invitation to the church to intensify social work aimed to facing the adverse conditions generated by the dynamics of the contemporary world. By this, the Centros de Información Social y Acción Social (Social Information and Social Action Centers)—CIAS—emerged, centers formed by highly quali-fied scientists. This instruction also indicated the need to create faculties of sociology taking advantage of the experience of the Society of Jesus in the university sphere and the wide academic circulation of "experts".

In Latin America, during the 1960s, the CIAS settled for the purpose of "(...) spreading and applying the social thought of the Church to the changing and explosive Latin American situation, in order to contribute to the necessary change of the social and economic structures of the conti-nent" (González, 1985, p. 235). The priest designated for the region was

Manuel Foyaca S.J. In Colombia, the CIAS began operating in 1966, as a replica of some experiences that had already been advanced in Europe, but with a separation from the ACC by setting a more investigative orientation. The direct advisor for Colombia was Pierre Bigo S.J. (Alejandro Angulo, 2020).

In 1968 the Instituto de Doctrina y Estudios Sociales (Institute of Doctrine and Social Studies)—IDES—was founded again on the initiative of the Colombian episcopate. The institute was also under the direction of the Jesuits and, as its name indicates, its objective was the dissemination of the social doctrine of the Church, while considering sociology as the ideal route to understand different social processes (Arias, 2003, pp. 249–250). Nevertheless, priests who devoted themselves to social research were taking another direction, one that went beyond strict religious frameworks. For example, in 1976 they changed the name of CIAS to CINEP—Centro de Investigación y Educación Popular (Centre for Popular Research and Education)—(González, 1998: 26–28). Misereor and Adveniat remained part of its funders.

To understand this experience of international Catholic cooperation, a case similar to the Colombian one was presented in Chile. Between 1947 and 1970, when the main processes of academic institutionalization of sociology occurred in Latin America, the Jesuits along with other communities, such as the Dominicans, had extended social analysis from the perspective of human development in the region. Among the most renowned European sociologists in this field were Joseph Fichter or Louis Lebret. Along these lines, the Centro para el Desarrollo Económico y Social de América Latina (Centre for the Economic and Social Development of Latin America), DESAL, and the Instituto Latinoamericano de Doctrina y Estudios Sociales (Latin American Institute of Doctrine and Social Studies) were established in Chile (Beigel, 2011, p. 15).

The trajectory followed by the Belgian priest Roger Vekemans is illustrative of the operation of these cooperation networks. He was the founder of the Chilean CIAS, of the School of Sociology at the Universidad Católica de Chile (Catholic University of Chile), of DESAL, and of the Centro Latinoamericano de Población y Familia (Latin American Center for Population and Family)—CELAP, in which Colombia participated through the ICODES led by the priest Gustavo Pérez; he also collaborated in the foundation of the Centro de Estudios e Investigaciones Sociales San Roberto Belarmino (San Roberto Belarmino Center for Social Studies and Research).

The case of DESAL stands out in this situation. The Centre, which began operating in 1960, was the regional office of Misereor and, in addition to the resources of this organization, it had others from Adveniat, the Vatican and the government of Belgium. The directive board was made up of people from Chile, Colombia, Ecuador, Venezuela and Bolivia. The main purpose of the organization was to advance scientific research that would contribute in a particular way to the social development of popular sectors and that, unlike the work carried out by CEPAL, would be guided by Christian humanism.

This popular promotion was functional to the objectives of other programs, such as the Alliance for Progress, when following strategies of containment of what, at the time, was read as the communist threat; but it was also of the rise of political forces such as the Christian Democracy in Chile and the mandate of Eduardo Frei Montalva (1964–1970). With the arrival of the government of Popular Unity of Salvador Allende (1970–1973), DESAL moved to Colombia opening its office in Bogota, which operated until 1990.

Other experiences that were born in the Society of Jesus, in the southern country, were the Centro de Investigación y Desarrollo de la Educación (Center for Research and Development of Education)—CIDE—in 1964 and the already mentioned ILADES in 1966. The activity of these groups was seriously affected by the military coup of Augusto Pinochet (Brunner, 1985) as it generally happened, during the Latin American dictatorships, with who worked in the area of social sciences.

In Colombia, Jesuits and Dominicans, in addition to their strong presence in the education field, already had renowned work in different communities and social sectors, based on social Christianity. There were important results in research processes that sought to promote the formulation of public and social policies, in the logic of social "development" that was desired for the region. The clearest example in the country, within the framework of what has been called tercermundismo católico (Catholic Third-World-ism), may be the Misión de Economía y Humanismo (Mission of Economy and Humanism) (1954–1958) led by Lebret; work considered by some researchers as a cardinal antecedent for the development of sociology in Colombia (Gómez, 2015).

The work, in its time, of the priest Gustavo Ramírez Pérez, who in 1959 created the Centro de Investigaciones Sociales (Center for Social Research)—CIS—as regional headquarters of the Federación Internacional de Investigaciones Sociales y Socioreligiosas (International Federation of

Social and Socio-religious Researches)—FERES, is another expression of such influence by the Order of Preachers. The CIS in turn manifests a particular form of research that was extended, for the social sciences, with Lebret's previous experience on Christian humanism, shared by those engaged in socio-religious studies.

It must not be forgotten that this development of international cooperation in Latin America must be framed in the geopolitical disputes of the Cold War. This is the only explanation for the important role played by organizations, mainly North American and Western European, in what was considered a way of countering the communist threat or attenuating the deplorable conditions resulting from unequal capitalist development. It is at this point that one finds the correspondence with experiences linked to Catholic Action, materialized in a diversity of clerical and lay organizations.

Thus, one can also understand the direct support offered by the United States through programs of the Alliance for Progress, such as the Peace Corps. Precisely Chile and Colombia received a large number of foreign volunteers who contributed with community work. In the first country, the Catholic Church became the basis for this action through Promoción Popular (Popular Promotion), while in the Colombian case it functioned through Acción Comunal (Communal Action) or Integración Popular (Popular Integration)" (Purcell, 2014, pp. 227–240).

Under this line the initial project of the sociologist Orlando Fals Borda was developed, who, along with others, sociologists and priests such as Camilo Torres Restrepo and Gustavo Pérez Ramírez, formed the Comité de Acción Comunal (Committee of Communal Action) under the Ministry of National Education. Colombia was the Latin American country that received the most Peace Corps volunteers. One of the most successful initiatives, and at the same time more known and studied, was overseen by the priest José Joaquín Salcedo with his work with Radio Sutatenza.

BIFURCATIONS ABOUT THE SOCIAL QUESTION

The "social question" was the axis that allowed the intertwining of the pastoral work of the Church with that which served as support, from other institutions, for the development of sociology in the country. While growing concerns about the unintended consequences of capitalist development were quickly supplanted by the fear of communism among the more conservative groups, the experience of approaching the community allowed the configuration of a critical perspective that interrogated the Christian vision of social change.

Another critical perspective was added to this one, that became central as the field of action of social sciences in Colombia expanded. The changing balance of power among various groups, in a country and a region with deep transformations in the 1960s, determined ruptures in the face of relative unanimity in the image built around the causes and consequences of the unequal development, characteristic of the prevailing economic and political system in the "West".

In Colombia, since the first third of the twentieth century, the Catholic Church was emphatic in its condemnation of popular movements, more if they explicitly expressed a relationship with the left. This condemnation, aimed at the autonomy that the grassroots organizations could gain, was the main engine for the creation of unions, cooperatives and other entities that had as a fundamental principle the defense of Christian morality, it was felt that social conflicts could be resolved through it. In the eyes of Catholicism, the problem was not social inequality, as was the moral crisis of contemporary society.

This idea supported the declaration of illegality of the Colombian Communist Party in 1954, during the government of General Gustavo Rojas Pinilla. In this administration, under a profoundly Catholic head of state, the social question was addressed from the perspective of assistentialism, closer to Christian charity. The most obvious example may be the formation of SENDAS, the Secretaria Nacional de Acción Social (National Secretariat for Social Action), which sought to serve marginalized sectors; or the creation of family subsidies due to the pressure exerted on businesses by Catholic unions (Arévalo, 2014, pp. 220–221).

One of the cases of direct relationship between the development of the social sciences and a certain religious ethos is provided by the program opened at the Pontificia Universidad Javeriana. This orientation, however, is not exclusive to denominational institutions since it is also partly recognized in the early years of the sociology program of the Universidad Nacional de Colombia (Restrepo, 2002, p. 88), where the meeting of those who were guided by a modern Christianity and those who defended the democratic-liberal development of the country took place (Jaramillo, 2017, pp. 236–237).

Several religious organizations worked as economic support for the extension of sociological work in the country, including the World Council of Churches and the Centro de Investigaciones Socio-Religiosas (Center for Socio-religious Research), along with those mentioned above. For the case of the Javeriana, in addition to cooperation centers such as UNESCO, USAID, among others, the Catholic networks had created a host of inter-disciplinary connections deployed in the field work. Some organizations that provided resources were the Catholic Medical Mission Board, the National Catholic Welfare Conference, the International Education Development or the Catholic Inter-American Cooperation Program—CICOP.

The network of universities was also important. Among those who contributed most during this period were the Catholic University of America, Woodstoock College, Fordham University and Saint Louis University,[2] without considering the training of a significant number of priests through student mobility. Likewise, the Javeriana had an accumulated experience thanks to the Cátedra Pontificia (Pontifical Lecture), which was open to courses from social doctrine of the Church to economy and humanism.

As extension activities, the work of the students in the *Unión Social Javeriana* (Javeriana Social Union), the Congregación Mariana Universitaria (Marian University Congregation) or the Instituto de Capacitación Obrera (Institute of Worker Training) was highlighted. One of the central antecedents for the creation of the sociology program in this university, along with that of social service, was the Instituto de Estudios Sociales (Institute of Social Studies) under the direction of Vicente Andrade Valderrama, S.J, one of the most active people in worker training courses and in the orientation of Catholic unions.

The close relationship with Catholic organizations could be interpreted as a mechanism that restrained or slowed down the possibilities of increasing the autonomy of the field of sociology in Colombia. Even so, for the Latin American case, this orientation was immersed in a political process that led to the growing interest in the social sciences and allowed sociological research to be channeled towards the most pressing problems of the country and the region. This is why these organizations contributed to the process of professionalization in the discipline (Cortés, 2021).

This effort did not allow the Church itself to perceive the changes that the region was experiencing and, in the face of which, the response of Catholic action did not arrive at effective solutions for disadvantaged

---

[2] Archivo histórico Javeriana (Javeriana's Historical Archive) -AHJ- AHJ- RFRM C12 D138 F 261, AHJ- RJER C17 D38 F96-99, AHJ- RJER C43 D61 F120-121, AHJ- RCOR C47 D12 F32-33)

groups. However, in the mid-1960s, this vision ended up taking an impressive turn for both the global Catholic Church and the active social movements in Latin America. Two facts have been widely recognized as triggers: the Second Vatican Council (1962–1965) and the Conference of Medellin (1968) organized by the Consejo Episcopal Latinoamericano (Latin American Episcopal Council)—CELAM—(Dussel, 1972, p. 173).

The Council, summoned during the pontificate of John XXIII, is the most direct expression of the Catholic Church's awareness of the need to rethink its place in society in the face of the evident and inevitable transformation of times. With an unusual defense of human rights, as well as a recognition of religious freedom, the council looked at the "social problem" with new lenses. At the same time, it promoted organizations among priests and laypeople to face this situation. The Conference of Medellin took the recommendations emanating from the Council but pointed out the need for a differentiated action in Latin America.

Despite these important foundations, the ecclesiastical hierarchy maintained deep reserves about the militancy that was raising in the accompaniment to the communities. Being one of the most conservative institutions in the region (Levine, 1985), from its hierarchy suspicion was manifested against the direction that followed pastoral work with an appeal to the social revolution, especially with the cultural, political and military influence the Cuban Revolution (1959) had. The path that can best express these contradictions, in the Colombian and Latin American socio-political context, may be that of the priest Camilo Torres Restrepo.

Once Torres entered the Major Seminary of Bogota after leaving law school, he founded, together with his friend Gustavo Pérez, the Círculo de Estudios Sociales (Social Studies Circle). As a member of the Order of Preachers, he studied at the School of Political and Social Sciences of the University of Louvain, a center in which several Latin American priests were trained with a deep concern for the social question (Beigel, 2011, pp. 98–100). He also created there, along with other students, the Equipo Colombiano de Investigación Socio Económica (Colombian Socio-Economic Research Team)—ECISE. He then attended some lectures in urban and labor sociology at the University of Minnesota.

His journey in the Dominican community clearly derives from the influence of works such as those of Lebret (Jaramillo, 2020, pp. 106–108) and in general from the experience of worker priests. From there he collected the ideas of certain advanced Catholicism represented in figures such as Emmanuel Mounier, Theilard de Chardin or Jaques Maritain

(Bernal, 2017). Co-founder of the sociology department of the Universidad Nacional de Colombia in 1959, as much of the researchers of the period, he was interested in working with the community, initially, under the predominant developmental perspective and its small-scale intervention orientation.

During his stay at the Universidad Nacional de Colombia, he served as an auxiliary chaplain. His closeness to students led him to participate with them in different mobilizations, at a time when the movement itself took on an unusual strength. Since then, he began to receive instructions from his superiors to abandon his religious habits. While he was a professor and researcher, he was also appointed director of the Escuela Superior de Administración Pública (Higher School of Public Administration)—ESAP, and made part of the Instituto de Reforma Agraria (Agrarian Reform Institute). Another important experience was his commitment to the foundation of the Movimiento Universitario de Promoción Comunal (University Movement for Community Promotion)—MUNIPROC— where action programs in this area were promoted.

His political commitment deepened as he inquired about the various obstacles that impeded social transformations which, as a Christian, he sought through his pastoral action and, as a social scientist, through sociological research (Levine, 2011). Thus, from accompanying different sectors (peasants, workers, students) in their demands, he decided to organize his own political movement, the Frente Unido (United Front), from where he hoped to overcome the democratic constraint forced by the National Front's model of government.

For Camilo, every Christian should make the revolution. Given that a defining element in national history had been violence, he oppositely proposed the idea of (insurgent) counterviolence as a form of legitimate action against the elite-operated power shutdown. This idea led him to join the Ejército de Liberación Nacional (National Liberation Army)— ELN, a guerrilla founded in 1965 with strong influence of the rebel movement that was victorious in the Cuban Revolution. He only lasted there four months, as he died in an ambush in February 1966 (Broderick, 2013). It is worth noting that other members of the church in Colombia joined guerrillas, including Domingo Laín, Manuel Pérez and José Antonio Jiménez; although this alternative never generated a consensus among their communities.

Torres represents the mixture between the revolutionary idealism of the time and the paternalism derived from Catholic action (Levine, 2011).

However, his expulsion from the Church before joining the guerrilla shows the contradictions between these two positions, contradictions characteristic of the ecclesiastical hierarchy but not of its bases, as a large number of priests trusted working side by side with impoverished sectors in the search for a profound transformation of the social structure. He saw in sociology the scientific strategy for making Christian love an "effective love".

In this direction there was also a rupture between the church and the different funding and support bodies, with the social science programs. In the first years of academic institutionalization, resources from international organizations allowed the creation of educational and research spaces in sociology. With the growing denunciation of cultural colonialism and with the force that the idea of anti-imperialist revolution took in the late 1960s, the fragile bond created with the international academic community was broken (Rudas, 2020, pp. 101–110).

Nevertheless, this type of experiences were fundamental in the development of other movements, such as the Liberation Theology (1971), current of great importance for Latin America. Mobility between different universities; the participation of several sociologist-priests in the CELAM, and their presence in different research groups such as FERES, especially under the direction of François Houtart (Pérez, 2022); DESAL and ILADES, among other facts, led to the thought that to achieve the desired changes it was necessary to know first the Latin American reality. Hence the importance of sociology as a suitable science for this purpose.

Movements of priests began to appear, taking up the social question as center of their action, but with a different orientation from that which had been outlined in its initial conception. This was influenced by the Political Theology of Johannes Metz (Espinosa, 2016, p. 138), the already mentioned worker priests or the grassroots community movement in Brazil in the late 1950s, which later in the region would mark the imprint with Rubén Alves's Theology of Hope. Also the works of Leonardo Boff and Gustavo Gutiérrez (Bernal, 2017, p. 133) until reaching the Movimiento de Sacerdotes para el Tercer Mundo (Movement of Priests for the Third World)—MSTM.

Problems related to "structural injustice and mass marginality" (González, 1985, p. 282), as diagnosis of the situation in the region, were understood not only as the issue to comprehend but on which to act. This is the basis of Liberation Theology in Latin America, and the Golconda movement in Colombia (Larosa, 2000, p. 26). Both movements, which were politically active and spread among the population, were rejected by the church hierarchy (Restrepo, 1995, pp. 27–37).

The particularity of readings like this run to no more talk on development. The new word, which involved different social movements, was that of liberation. It is the religious tone mentioned above, or the derivative of the revolutionary discourse of anti-imperialism: this was the new objective that was configured in view of the defining characteristics of the region. Thus, the reformist vision of developmentalism was abandoned by social sciences, which led to a profound change in the way sociology had been conceived.

The variations in the organization of the discipline went hand in hand with the strength that the student movement was acquiring by the late 1960s. Along with the search for a greater participation of students in institutional decisions and their strong criticism of the democratic closure resulting from the National Front, there were the demands that most affected the way as, until then, sociology had developed in the country in some of the university training programs that were already operating.

On the one hand, the reformist vision with small-scale interventions began to generate resistance because it allowed maintaining or expanding the state of inequality and inequity characteristic of the region, and even more of a country like Colombia. On the other hand, foreign aid that had functioned as an economic and scientific support began to be judged under the suspicion of imperialist intervention, an intervention that contributed to the condition of domination of Latin America.

Reaction against this position was not minor. In addition to the change in perception of the student body that started being considered a dangerous critical stratum, especially at a time when insurgent groups fed their ranks with people from this sector, the containment of the expansion of the left came to be with increasingly coercive and violent measures. In the case of sociology programs at denominational universities, the situation proved to be more dramatic.

The first program to close was at Pontificia Universidad Javeriana, in 1972. Years later the same situation would occur in other institutions of higher education. From there a halo of suspicion was built around discipline, which no longer seemed a natural ally of the reformist attempts from above. On the contrary, it had become a staunch critique of how, from the elites, inequality and violence that characterized the country deepened.

These changes in academia led to sociology, as a research sphere par excellence, moved from universities to research centers that were beginning to consolidate, such as the CINEP; or that many of the academics who graduated from the Universidad Nacional de Colombia mainly, were concerned with returning some empirical orientation to the discipline when opening new programs. However, the creation of new spaces of inquiry, dissemination, training and debate continued to grow in the following decades.

REFERENCES

Archila, M. (1991). *Cultura e identidad obrera. Colombia 1910–1945.* Cinep.
Archila, M. (2008). *Idas y venidas. Vueltas y revueltas. Protestas sociales en Colombia 1958–1990.* Icanh-Cinep.
Arévalo, D. (2014). Crecimiento económico y protección social, dos patrones divergentes en Colombia. Una mirada a partir de la acción gubernamental, 1930–1967. In F. Purcell & R. Arias (Eds.), *Chile-Colombia: diálogos sobre sus trayectorias históricas* (pp. 203–225). Ediciones Uniandes.
Arias, R. (2003). *El episcopado colombiano: intransigencia y laicidad (1850–2000).* Ceso-Universidad de los Andes-ICANH.
Arriaga, M. (2013). Una nueva misión para una vieja iglesia. Redes católicas de ayuda humanitaria. In T. Kuri, & M. Arriagada (Comp.), *El fin de un sueño secular: religión y relaciones internacionales en el cambio de siglo* (pp. 35–68). El colegio de México.
Beigel, F. (2011). *Misión Santiago. El mundo académico jesuita y los inicios de la cooperación internacional católica.* LOM Editores.
Beltrán, J. (2018). *Cuando se borró el nombre de Dios: Laureano Gómez, Félix Restrepo S.J. y el corporativismo colombiano (1930–1964).* Tesis pregrado Fac. Ciencias Sociales. PUJ.
Bernal, I. (2017). Influencia del Movimiento de Curas Obreros en América Latina. *Revista Estudios del Desarrollo Social: Cuba y América Latina, 5*(2), 130–139. http://scielo.sld.cu/scielo.php?script=sci_abstract&pid=S2308-01 322017000200012&lng=pt&nrm=iso
Bidegain, A. (1985). *Iglesia, pueblo y política. Estudios de conflicto e intereses. Colombia 1930–1955.* PUJ.
Broderick, W. (2013). *Camilo, el cura guerrillero.* Ícono.
Brunner, J. (1985). La participación de los centros académicos privados. *Estudios Públicos, 19,* 1–12. https://estudiospublicos.cl/index.php/cep/article/view/1722

Cifuentes, M. (2010). Partidos políticos de influencia católica. El caso del Partido Demócrata Cristiano en Colombia. *Ciudad paz-ando, 3*(2), 26–38. https://doi.org/10.14483/2422278X.7348

Cortés, A. (2021). Clodomiro Almeyda and Roger Vekemans: The tension between autonomy and political commitment in the institutionalization of Chilean sociology, 1957–1973. *Current sociology, 69*(6), 900–918. https://doi.org/10.1177/0011392120932935

Cortés, J. (1997). Regeneración, intransigencia, y régimen de cristiandad. *Historia Crítica, 15*, 3–12. https://doi.org/10.7440/histcrit15.1997.00

Dussel, E. (1972). *Historia de la Iglesia en América Latina*. Ed. Nova Terra.

Escudero, J. (1997). El pontificado de Achille Ratti, papa Pío XI. *Anuario de Historia de la Iglesia, No.*, 6, 77–112. https://revistas.unav.edu/index.php/anuario-de-historia-iglesia/article/view/24749

Espinosa, J. (2016). Johann Baptist Metz y la teología cristiana "después de Auschwitz". *Cuestiones Teológicas, 43*(99), 133–147. https://doi.org/10.18566/cueteo.v43n99.a06

Gómez, J. (2015). *El trabajo de la Misión de Economía y Humanismo en Colombia 1954–1958*. Tesis de Pregrado, PUJ.

González, F. (1985). La doctrina social de la Iglesia frente a las ciencias sociales: intentos y dificultades de un diálogo". *Theologica Xaveriana*. No. 75 Año 35/2, 235–289. https://revistas.javeriana.edu.co/index.php/teoxaveriana/article/view/22364

González, F. (1998). La experiencia del CINEP: una escuela de investigadores. In F. González (Ed.), *Una opción y muchas búsquedas. CINEP 25 años* (pp. 23–62). Cinep.

Jaramillo, J. (2017). *Estudiar y hacer sociología en Colombia en los años sesenta*. Ediciones Universidad Central.

Jaramillo, J. (2020). Los orígenes de la sociología profesional en Colombia: Camilo Torres, proyección académica, investigación científica y actividad social y política (1959–1964). S. Vanegas (Coord.). In *Trayectorias y proyectos intelectuales. El pensamiento social en América Latina y Colombia* (pp. 104–128). PUJ.

Larosa, M. (2000). *De la derecha a la izquierda: historia de la iglesia católica en Colombia 1930–1980*. Fundación para la promoción de la investigación y la tecnología.

Levine, D. H. (1985). Continuities in Colombia. *Journal of Latin American Studies, 17*(2), 295–317.

Levine, D. H. (2011). Camilo Torres: Fe, Política y Violencia. *Sociedad y religión, 21*(34–35)http://www.scielo.org.ar/sciclo.php?script=sci_arttext&pid=S1853-70812011000100004

Montero, F. (2005). Origen y evolución de la acción católica española. In A. Villaverde, A. Botti, & J. de la Cueva (Coord.), *Clericalismo y asociacionismo católico en España, de la Restauración a la Transición: un siglo entre el palio y el consiliario* (pp. 133–159). Universidad de Castilla.

Navarro, G. (2013). Catholic International Cooperation: Social research in the Society of Jesus. In F. Beigel (Ed.), *The politics of academic autonomy in Latin America*. Routledge. https://bookshelf.vitalsource.com/#/books/978131 7020585/

Pérez, J. (2022). Modernidad religiosa, acción cultural pastoral y cooperación internacional católica en Medellín 1959–1969. *Revista colombiana de sociología., 45*(1), 45–68. https://doi.org/10.15446/rcs.v45n1.90235

Plata, W. (2013). El sindicato del servicio doméstico y la Obra de Nazareth. Entre asistencialismo, paternalismo y conflicto de interés, Bogotá (1938–1960). *Revista de Estudios Sociales, No., 45*, 29–41. https://doi.org/10.7440/res45.2013.03

Purcell, F. (2014). El Cuerpo de Paz y el desafío del desarrollo en perspectiva transnacional: Chile y Colombia en la década de 1960. In F. Purcell & R. Arias (Eds.), *Chile-Colombia: diálogos sobre sus trayectorias históricas* (pp. 227–247). Ediciones Uniandes.

Restrepo, G. (2002). *Peregrinación en pos de omega: sociología y sociedad en Colombia*. UN.

Restrepo, J. (1995). *La revolución de las sotanas*. Planeta.

Roitman, M. (2008). *Pensar América Latina. El desarrollo de la sociología latino-americana*. Marcos Roitman Rosenmann. Clacso.

Rudas, N. (2020). *Ciencia y revolución: el Departamento de Sociología en la Universidad Nacional de Colombia (1967–1971)*. Tesis de Maestría, Universidad de los Andes.

INTERVIEWS

Alejandro Angulo, S. J. February – 2020. Bogotá.

CHAPTER 5

Ruptures and Continuities in Contemporary Colombian Sociology

Abstract This chapter provides an overview of the current development of sociology in Colombia. For this, it begins with an approach to two topics that have concentrated much of the intellectual production in the area: the studies of violence and armed conflict, and the Investigación Acción Participativa. The first concerns one of the long-standing major social problems on the national territory. The second, an original and genuine attempt to configure an owned science, an attempt that gave some renown to Colombian sociology at the regional level.

Then, the contemporary configuration process of the field of sociology in the country is explored. By drawing on the experience of professionals of different generations, an image is built around the pedagogical, investigative, employment, and activist work of those who have opted for sociology as a career. Based on interviews with its protagonists, some reflections on the possibilities and obstacles facing the discipline today are presented. At the same time, it leaves open routes from which to continue contributing to the resolution of our most pressing and relevant problems.

Keywords Studies of violence • Investigación Acción Participativa • Colombian sociology • Post-agreement

© The Author(s), under exclusive license to Springer Nature Switzerland AG 2023
J. Aldana Cedeño, *Sociology in Colombia*, Sociology Transformed,
https://doi.org/10.1007/978-3-031-39412-6_5

Taking 1959 as the year in which the process of academic institutionaliza-tion of sociology began in Colombia, the production derived from research activity in the area barely exceeds 60 years. Although previous studies were carried out with an orientation that could be described as sociological, as presented in Chap. 2, it would not be until the creation of training pro-grams in different universities that, jointly, progress would made in a type of research that tried to catch up with discipline in other parts of the world.

During these years, due to the very nature of sociology, the issues that have dominated the inquiry agenda respond directly to the most pressing problems or situations that must be faced by the country. It is therefore not surprising that sociologists are interested in understanding and acting on the conditions that generate the overflowing violence that has charac-terized the long Colombian armed conflict. At the same time, it is not surprising the high socio-political commitment these professionals have acquired, given their proximity to the most affected social sectors when they have not themselves been the object of aggressive demonstrations against their work.

However, if studies on violence have had an important production since the end of the 1960s, for the same period other fields linked to the so-called specialized sociologies will be unfolded: rural, urban, political, industrial and work, of culture, of science, of gender, just to mention a few. There was also an early self-reflective exercise that led to a constant review of the discipline's development, its place according to the differen-tiated regional configuration in the country and its relationship with diverse groups thanks to its possibilities for action in the short, medium, and long term.

VIOLENCE(S) AND ARMED CONFLICT

Among the investigations that demarcated the sociological knowledge widespread in the country, in the process of its institutionalization, those advanced by Orlando Fals Borda in the middle of the 1950s are recog-nized. These express the tone of the relationship that was initially estab-lished between scientific practice and its social impact through public policy; but they also exemplify the effort to achieve, through a rigorous exercise, a scientific knowledge that surpasses the usual "essayism" that until that moment had characterized the analysis of social reality (Obregón, 1987).

Tabio, estudio de la organización social rural (Tabio, a study of the rural social organization) (Lynn, 1944) or *Peasant society in the Colombian Andes: a sociological study of the Saucio* (Fals, 1955), were texts that marked one of the most fruitful trends in sociology with rural studies (Vega, 2012, p. 253). This problematic could not be understood, however, without examining the changes brought by the advance of urbanization in several regions, reason why urban sociology was also a field of interest that led to numerous investigations during this period. Texts such as *La proletarización de Bogotá: Ensayo de metodología estadística* (The proletarianization of Bogota: Essay on statistical methodology) (Torres, 1961) by Camilo Torres correspond to preliminary concerns about the abrupt transformations, many of them violent, suffered by the peasantry, one of the most vulnerable populations in Colombia.

Between these two topics the initial inquiries that brought together teachers and students in multiple research projects began. With the support of various public and private entities, sociology was finding a space in which its "experts" connected directly with opportunities to influence, through public policy, in different social areas. Soon, the interests that guided the participation of this scientific community, moved towards the theme that has marked an imprint in the history of sociology in Colombia, namely, violence and their different expressions in the long armed conflict.

In Chap. 3, *La Violencia in Colombia* (Violence in Colombia) was mentioned as one of the emblematic texts, both for the emergence of discipline in the country, and for the construction of the vision on it that would be predominant among public opinion, especially because of the rejection of its findings by political parties, the armed forces, and some media. By the mid-1960s, when the book was published, one could not foresee how the bloody events of recent history would mark the path followed by the long armed conflict still raging in the country, the longest in the western hemisphere.

This document was the first systematic attempt to account for a phenomenon of such magnitude, present in various regions of the country, with the voice of different actors involved, civilians and armed, and drawing on all available sources at the time. Without establishing exact figures on the loss of human life, material dispossession, migration, and the breakdown of the social fabric in the peasant world, the analysis marked several lines of research that determined the particularity of Colombian sociology. Among one of the conclusions that would later be widely discussed, Fals Borda spoke of the "institutionalization of dysfunction", in which the action of formal institutions ended up feeding violence (Guzmán et al., 1962, pp. 401–404).

Violences like these intensified and degraded as the number of armed actors also increased, with a devastating outcome that, in principle, had as its epicenter the rural environment, but that was spreading in the cities revealing new manifestations. That sociology that in its academic beginnings had as its horizon the intervention on a small scale, and that had the support of governmental instances and the ecclesiastical hierarchy, among other institutions, was disappearing. Between 1960 and 1970 another orientation was configured aimed to constructing a critical sociology that stuck its finger on the wound around the relevant issues and, therefore, assigned responsibilities that until now had gone unnoticed.

In this period, amid the structuring of intervention policies throughout Latin America generated in the framework of the Cold War, tensions between the different groups in conflict spread to other spheres. On the social level, the containment of the left occurred with such vehemence that its militants became considered the "internal enemy". On the academic level, classrooms became spaces in dispute for the construction of the legitimate vision of the social order, as well as of the defense of the correct political posture when understanding that order. Finally, the one that prevailed was the one that advocated for the anti-imperialist and anti-colonialist struggle.

The different sociology programs thus proposed profound transformations in the teaching of the discipline as well as in the development of the research that was then considered appropriate. Having as a priority political commitment, characterized by the idea of national liberation, and working together with the best organized sectors such as the student-workers and the peasants, the role of science was assumed from the responsibility to understand but, above all, to act to contribute to the structural changes required by Colombian society.

In the midst of the formation of several insurgent groups, sociologists tried to generate resources to support the processes carried out by social movements. Among these resources, the reconstruction of the trajectories followed in organizational projects made possible the promotion of the practice of historicizing popular struggles, which did not yet have records or appeared in official sources. This happened with peasant leagues, left-wing groups, and workers' associations (Sánchez, 2004, p. 42).

The 1980s were the stage on which studies on violence expanded, deepened and diversified. Amid the fluctuations of the guerrilla organizations, some that remained for decades, among them the Fuerzas Armadas Revolucionarias de Colombia (Revolutionary Armed Forces of Colombia)—FARC, or are still maintained, although with a different ideological character, such as the Ejército de Liberación Nacional (National Liberation Army)—ELN, and others who demobilized, such as the Movimiento 19 de Abril (April 19th Movement)—M-19, paramilitary groups emerged. The blend between civilian population, business circles, local politicians, drug cartels and members of the State, which converged in the counterinsurgency doctrine, found in the enormous resources of drug trafficking the fuel that unleashed the horror that the country would live since then.

Faced with an exacerbated violence and a relentless persecution of people or groups that drew attention to it, in these years a line of inquiry emerged, driven mostly by sociologists. The "violentólogos" ("violentologists") managed to consolidate a research agenda that not only deepened the analysis of the armed conflict, but also provided alternatives for overcoming it. Although this line was later criticized for placing the explanation of the conflict in its "objective" causes (Blair, 2005), it opened the discussion on the real weight of political violence, which turned out to be very low compared to other manifestations, such as violence in the "streets" (Comisión de estudios sobre la violencia, 1987, p. 18).

Among the outstanding researchers are those who had as a point of convergence the Instituto de Estudios Políticos y Relaciones Internacionales (Institute of Political Studies and International Relations)—IEPRI—created in 1986 at the Universidad Nacional de Colombia. Its official publication, the journal *Análisis político* (Political Analysis), collects the most important production generated during these years (Pécaut, 1998). As a group, the space opened during the government of Virgilio Barco (1986–1990) in the Comisión para la Superación de la Violencia (Commission for the Overcoming of Violence) (1987), worked to strengthen their project. The results and recommendations are found in the book *Colombia, violencia y democracia* (Colombia, Violence and Democracy) (1987).

Gonzalo Sánchez Gómez, Álvaro Camacho Guizado, Eduardo Pizarro Leongómez or Carlos Eduardo Jaramillo, members of the aforementioned commission, are among those who have developed their professional trajectories based on studies of violence, extending the framework of understanding of the phenomenon. Camacho, for example, together with Álvaro Guzmán Barney, inquired about urban violence along with other consequences that had brought the strengthening of drug trafficking, the actions of drug cartels and the failed anti-drug policy (Camacho & Guzmán, 1990).

Some of the documents that give an account of the work done in this area are *Al filo del caos: crisis política en la Colombia de los años 80* (On the edge of chaos: political crisis in Colombia in the 1980s) (Leal & Zamosc, 1990) and *Pacificar la paz* (Pacify peace) (Reyes, 1992). Many other names are associated with this field of research that has generated a vast bibliography. In the case of sociology, with a permanent production and an impact on academia or public opinion, the voices of Francisco Leal Buitrago, Fernando Cubides, Alejandro Reyes (Restrepo, 2002, pp. 172–173), William Ramirez, appear among many others who have advanced their inquiries in this field.

Both because of the trajectories of these researchers, and because of the source of the resources that were drew for the research, this work began reducing the enormous distance that had been opened between the government and the social sciences. It made it possible to make people understand that there were many forms of violence, *many violences*, and that, qualified as political, only represented a small percentage. As a result, several studies, research, and project centers emerged, such as the Banco de Datos sobre Derechos Humanos y Violencia Política (Human Rights and Political Violence Data Bank) (1987), the most complete in Colombia, of the Centro de Investigación y Educación Popular (Center for Research and Popular Education)—Cinep—and the Comisión Intercongrecacional de Justicia y Paz (Inter-Congregational Commission for Justice and Peace) (Jaramillo Marín, 2011).

However, outside the sphere of the so-called violentologists, the work of Alfredo Molano is an essential reference when understanding the Colombian armed conflict and its multiple dimensions. Through social biographies, life trajectories of people who have been protagonists or have suffered the assaults of violence under the particularities of regional fragmentation that characterizes Colombia, Molano built the history of the conflict from below. Among many of his titles in this direction *Los bombardeos de El Pato* (The Bombings of El Pato) (Molano & Resyes, 1980), *Los años del tropel: relatos de violencia* (The years of Turmoil: Stories of Violence) (Molano, 1985); *Siguiendo el corte: relatos de guerras y de* tierras (Following the Cut: Stories of Wars and Lands) (Molano, 1989) *and Trochas y fusiles* (Trails and Guns) (Molano, 1994) appear.

The study on violence, however, has been separated from the exclusive analysis around the Colombian armed conflict. Addressing territorial inequalities, for example, or opening the spectrum to other questions closer to human rights or the need for intersectional studies, certainly is the result of the accumulation of quite a lot of decades of research on the subject. The participation of sociologists in the processes of clarification, truth, justice, and reparation continues to be active, with a commitment that has historically gone through the exercise of discipline in the country.

Investigación Acción Participativa: IAP

Another of the lines that has preserved an importance for sociology in the country is the Investigación Acción Participativa (participatory action research). Although it does not offer the dimension of academic and research production that has been pointed out for studies on violence and conflict, its representativeness at the regional level has positioned it as one of the most interesting contributions facing the historical particularities of Latin America and, therefore, as a relevant mechanism to address, in a situated way, our problems. Among its promoters Fals Borda is recognized although, being consistent with the spirit that animates this project, the road has been traveled collectively, with ramifications not entirely recorded due to the indistinction between scientific work and social activism.

As an initial proposal, it is paradoxical that at the time when Fals Borda was accused of being a friendly agent of imperialism, in particular for his effective work on funding matters and for the establishment of international cooperation networks for the nascent sociology department of the Universidad Nacional de Colombia (Rudas, 2019), he himself was opening the space for the development of a field of knowledge politically committed and active with national problems. He bet himself on a sociology that would escape intellectual colonialism.

As its name indicates, the IAP was constituted in a special way to advance research by the hand of social activism. For this reason, this work does not extend on any social group, it occurs in the particular space in which subordinate sectors are located, in which human beings live under conditions of domination and exclusion. The objective, in addition to meeting the needs and demands of these sectors, is to enter and deepen the way in which, from there, owned visions of the world are built.

The relationship between scientific and popular knowledge, or people's science, is then posed horizontally. Although stated as this, they would seem to be two different and separate areas. What is sought is to make them converge towards a same direction that leads to the construction of "una ciencia propia", an owned science (Correa, 2016, p. 229); a science that counteracts intellectual colonialism from which counterproductive policies for the political, cultural and economic autonomy of Latin America emerge.

It was thus possible to design a proposal based on participatory research, with a pre-eminence of collaborative methodologies. The best example that illustrates an attempt of this type is perhaps *Historia Doble de la Costa* (Double History of the Coast) (1979–1987) with the two explanatory channels, written by Fals Borda, which parallelly travel the reconstruction of the regional history of the Colombian Caribbean. Besides exposing the search for materials and conceptions typical of the inhabitants of the region, as well as collecting the trajectory of popular struggles, it is also a good example of the purpose of decentralizing sociology, removing it from urban centers, and placing it in everyday debates rather than proper academic ones (Fals, 2002).

As a methodology, the IAP seeks to "produce radical changes in society" (Fals, 1980, p. 149), therefore it is sustained on a scientific-political purpose. While it is a question of establishing practical objectives, the process that follows is more interesting than the result, since the collaborative work with communities allows achieving transformations in the forms of thought and in the ways of acting that have become common. The configuration of an "emerging science or culture" is thus expected which, on other occasions, has been expressed under the characteristics of "popular wisdom".

In Fals's own words, "it is understood (as) the empirical knowledge, practical, common sense, which has been ancestral cultural and ideological possession of the people of the social bases, the one that has allowed them to create, work and interpret predominantly with the direct resources that nature offers to man" (Fals, 1980, p. 152). This perspective has sometimes made IAP more of an epistemology than a methodology.

Nonetheless, it reserves certain conditions that are expected to be followed in each new investigative process: authenticity in the commitment to accompany the popular movements; anti-dogmatism; systematic return of knowledge to the community in order to support social changes; return to engaged intellectuals to revise their own scientific bases; transition from reflection to action, and preservation of a "modest science and dialogical techniques".

This effort exceeded a strictly sociological perspective. To the interdisciplinary practice, between sociology, history and anthropology, the confluence of different knowledges was added. Oral tradition and the so-called archive trunks, as reservoirs of local knowledge, were part of the "simple techniques" used by the investigative teams. Collaborators of different origins were integrated in the creation of new communication strategies trying to bridge the enormous distance that, by other methods, had been established between object-subject (Anzola, 1990, pp. 99–102).

In spite of the intention of constituting an interdisciplinary practice, it was thought to create a proper or owned sociology, since the one inherited from Europe and the United States tended to a social development quite different from the one that determined the singularity of Latin America and in general, of the global south: the condition of colonization. With a view to consolidating a Latin American sociology, the First IAP World Symposium was held in Cartagena in 1977. 7 years earlier, through the La Rosca Foundation, this process had already begun. Colombia, Brazil, Mexico, Venezuela, India and Tanzania were some of the places where several collectives were reflecting on this trend (Rappaport, 2021).

This convergence is partly understood because, between 1960 and 1970, many countries in the region faced similar difficulties arising from the North American pressure to control different social movements, movements that advocated profound transformations of the social system in force at that time. During these years it was not uncommon for social sciences professionals, as well as Latin American intellectuals and artists, to advance their respective work by enunciating a social commitment close to left-wing ideas (Gilman, 2003). In fact, although anti-dogmatism was defended, Marxism served as a fundamental basis for the practice and theorization of the IAP.

This committed research experience continued to extend beyond the academy. Whether it was in the processes that occurred in the 1970s linked to popular education, close to the ideas of the Brazilian Paulo Freire, or those already mentioned on the subject of the increasingly used collaborative methodologies in social sciences, IAP has functioned as a mechanism for co-construction of knowledge in the communities themselves. Hence derives the potential of its exercise in contemporary sociological practice.

OPENNESS AND DIVERSITY IN SOCIOLOGICAL INTERESTS

These two lines have been decisive in the development of sociological knowledge in Colombia, but they have not been the only ones. With historical and generational fluctuations, different themes appear that have opened other veins of exploration and, some of them, already present an important production in their respective fields. Although some of these themes have been mentioned in Chap. 3, some of them appear again here, but now privileging the voices of their own protagonists.[1]

Perhaps one of the most relevant aspects, strengthened in the last three decades, has been the effort to "decentralize" sociology, both in teaching opportunities and in the definition of a research agenda. The creation of the first programs in Bogota and Medellin allowed the broaden the view on the problems arising from the rapid and abrupt process of urbanization that took place in the middle of the twentieth century. However, this process could not be understood without taking into account the situation of the rural world, which made it necessary to direct the lens towards the regions at an early stage.

The opening of new training centers in other major cities, but especially in intermediate cities, diversified the spectrum of problems under study in the discipline. Through situated research, phenomena closely linked to the rurality and the peasantry, for example the colonization,[2] became of interest precisely to understand the social, political, and economic changes in the regional configuration of the country.

Thanks to these new centers, research has been consolidated on the particular problems of the Afro-Colombian population,[3] with emphasis on the Pacific region[4] and the indigenous population[5] in the south-western

---

[1] The following reflection derives from the results of the research project "The sociocultural field of Colombian sociology (1960–2010). An approach from trajectories of sociologist". In it, the trajectory of 50 sociologists has been reconstructed, covering all the generations that have been trained in higher education programs since the 1960s. Likewise, particular attention has been paid to those who develop their activity inside and outside the universities covering the entire national territory.

[2] These are some of the problems investigated by Gloria Rivas, Fernando Urrea and Jaime E. Jaramillo. See Jaramillo et al. (1986).

[3] See Barbary and Urrea (2004). Central to this direction is the work of Betty Ruth Lozano based on black feminist epistemology.

[4] Espinosa (2011).

[5] This is the case of Gloria Rivas. In addition to being a researcher, she worked in different entities, including as a promoter of Indigenous Affairs in San Rafael de Planas (Meta)

part of Colombia. Likewise, those who were pioneers in vindicating studies in the area of culture were the sociologists who were developing their work on the Caribbean coast. From there, production around the carnival and popular festivals[6] was expanded to other areas.

One of the fields in which there have been profound modifications, not only for what has been built around in terms of research, theory, and action with communities, but what it has meant as a critical review of sociology itself and the constitution of emerging epistemological and methodological paths, are gender studies. Although in previous chapters it had already been pointed out how this was a work driven by women like Anita Rico, Rafaela Obeso, Magdalena León or Nohra Segura, to mention only some names, in contemporary sociology new perspectives are exhibited in the direction indicated.

However, these activities continue to be underreported. Although women were responsible for the pioneering studies on women themselves in relation to family or domestic work, their representativeness in dissemination bodies, especially in scientific journals (García, 2018), and their recognition in the process of institutionalization of sociology in Colombia, is less than the space that has been legitimized for the production derived from sociological work among men.

On the one hand, priority attention to the conflict, in relation to the role of the State and the various actors involved, lost sight for a time of the problems linked to private life, sexuality or religiosity, in general, matters commonly associated with the constitution of the symbolic (Uricoechea, 2001). On the other hand, the same condition of women between the 1960s and 1990s, in the usual tension between the world of work and family in which maternity is confined, a tension that continues in the academic and research field, has exerted unequal pressure on vocational training and job performance opportunities.

In contemporary sociology, giving continuity largely to the experience in research and theorization initiated by Luz Gabriela Arango or by anthropologist Mara Viveros, particularly in the *Escuela de Género* (Gender School), there are the different projects of the sociologists Alanis Bello and Ange La Furcia, who also unfold in social activism. Reflecting on the sociology of care, they are committed to situated research that addresses social problems from the body and emotions. From there one of them proposes new methodologies that are also translated into her work as an

[6] See Rey (2000).

educator using feminist pedagogies. The results in terms of production and dissemination go beyond the traditional academic frameworks that have been established for what can be considered scientific.

Sociology in these cases, due to its possibilities to understand the logics that support and explain the organization of the world, has also contributed with the elaboration of self-reflective exercises for the understanding of deprivation, discrimination, violence and exclusion suffered at structural and personal levels. This understanding, the basis of activism, has been fundamental not only for the communities with which it interacts, but also has occupied a central place in the practice of sociologists who have faced these challenges.

This accumulated research, which could be described as fruitful in the 60 years of sociology in Colombia as a delimited professional field, time considered in turn since its academic institutionalization, has occurred in its majority precisely among those who have worked as teachers in the various higher education programs. With the existence of some research centers, funding possibilities are now concentrated in academic spaces, with management facilitated through universities.

Classrooms have also provided one of the permanent job opportunities for sociologists. Despite the closures of several programs between the 1970s and 1980s, with the creation of new ones or the reopening of a few between the 1990s and the first decade of this century, the formation of new generations has been constituted as a moderately stable possibility to be able to live of the profession. However, there are few teaching positions, which ends up complicating the situation of labor precariousness that accompanies the hiring by hours system, both in the universities themselves as with the "service provision contracts" in various entities.[7]

Another of the spaces in which sociology as a craft has occupied a relevant place are the governmental instances. Among these are the municipal administrations either in the secretariats of education, culture, or public media, and in national institutions such as the Instituto Colombiano de Bienestar Familiar (Colombian Family Welfare Institute), the Departamento nacional de Planeación (National Planning Department) or the Ministry of Education.[8] In terms of impact on public policy, one

---

case in which a sociological perspective was favored was the Observatorio de Cultura Ciudadana (Citizen Culture Observatory) created during the first Mayor's term of Antanas Mockus (1995–1997) in Bogota.

Between Peace Processes and the Post-agreement

As recorded in the first section of this chapter, sociology in Colombia has had as its action framework the prolonged armed conflict, along with the various historical manifestations of violence in the country. With different effects depending on the region, this phenomenon is present in training exercises, research practice, social activism, and job opportunities for those who decide to dedicate themselves to this profession.

Before presenting in a general way some experiences around the performance of sociologists in this field, it is important to note that the damages related to threats, disappearances, expulsions, and incarcerations, have not been minor. Thus, from those who openly militated in leftist movements and witnessed the extermination of an entire political party, the Unión Patriótica (Patriotic Union), between 1984 and the 1990s; those who had to face prison[9] because they were perceived as sympathizers of insurgent groups; those who were forced to leave the country by threats[10]; to those who tired of this situation decided to continue their studies abroad, the violence is not only a phenomenon to analyze. It has also been one of the blows suffered by the sociological exercise in the country.

This situation becomes even more complex in the face of what working with affected communities has meant. From region to region, or from case to case, the selective assassinations and massacres among the inhabitants, accompanying the search and reparation processes, question the limits of sociology itself. The heartbreaking stories that feed the memory exercises, as well as forcing us to overcome partial visions from the classification between good and bad, also bring with them uncalculated and untreated damages to the physical, emotional, and psychological health of the researchers.

---

[9] It is the experience of Miguel Ángel Beltrán, who has been in this situation on 3 occasions.
[10] Alfredo Molano, Álvaro Camacho, Eduardo Pizarro, among others suffered exile. One of the cases declared as a crime against humanity is the murder of Alfredo Correa de Andreis. Luis Fernando Lalinde, a sociology student who was forcefully disappeared and was extrajudicially executed by members of the security forces in 1984, was the first disappeared person in the country recognized by the Inter-American Commission on Human Rights. These are perhaps the best-known cases, unfortunately they are not the only ones.

Still, the conflict's scenarios remain one of the places where social scientists test their capabilities in the area. From a laboratory for training in the discipline, such as the peace negotiations between the government of Andrés Pastrana (1998–2002) and the FARC in San Vicente del Caguán, to direct participation in studies around the different phases of the conflict, these spaces have allowed the diversification of the lines of research that nourish Colombian sociology.

In the texts derived from the analyses carried out in commissions on violence and armed conflict, along with the recording of the facts, alternatives have been proposed to overcome this situation. For example, in the previously mentioned research that gave rise to the book *Colonización, coca y guerrilla* (Colonization, coca and guerrrilla) (Jaramillo et al., 1986), with the investigation into colonization and the expansion that drug trafficking showed, the advantages of crop substitution or the management of Zonas de Reserva Campesina (Peasant reserve areas) began to be discussed.

In recent times, other sociologists have actively intervened not only in research processes, but also in others that have to do with reparation and memory construction. The participation of Álvaro Camacho in three of the main commissions of studies on violence, in 1958, 1987 and in the historical memory group organized by the Comisión Nacional de Reparación y Reconciliación (National Commission for Reparation and Reconciliation) in 2005 (Valencia, 2015), exemplifies one of many trajectories of people who have performed in this field.

Eduardo Pizarro himself, along with Gonzalo Sanchez, was on the Comisión Nacional de Reparación, assigned as its president in 2005. At another point in his professional career, he accompanied the laying down arms process of the M-19, a guerrilla whose commander was his own brother, Carlos Pizarro. With his work he has tried to shape a sociology of the guerrilla, given the particularities of the Colombian case around the confluence of different ideological currents in the different insurgent groups that formed in the country (Pizarro, 1996).

In relation to this new commitment enunciated at the end of the previous section, is the work of Alanis Bello in the *Centro Nacional de Memoria Histórica* (National Center of Historical Memory). She was in charge of the report on sexual violence in the context of the armed conflict as well as a study on LGBTI groups in Tolima. She also advised those at the helm of other reports on this particular subject. Adriana Bonilla participated in the Truth Commission, the first to exists in Colombia, in charge of the Pacific Chapter of the territorial volume. One of the commissioners, in charge of the macroregion of the Orinoquia, was Alfredo Molano.

Resulting of the partial agreement of Havana (2015) built once the cycle of peace negotiations between the government of Juan Manuel Santos (2010–2018) and the FARC was closed, some optimism before the possibility of configuring a post-conflict sociology was generated. Today, in taking up the proposal that was endorsed in the Cartagena Agreement (2016) after several years of non-implementation of the points agreed there, perhaps it's better to talk about the "*posacuerdo*", the post-agreement. With it all, in what has been understood as effects of these dialogues, the openness to other concerns of civil society reopens the question of the spaces that sociology should occupy in Colombia.

In the years 2019 and 2021, the social upheaval revealed a profound change in the way of dealing with social inconformities. Without any recent precedent, a national strike was organized that summoned a significant number of people, of different origins, with the taking of the streets in towns and cities. Young people became the main protagonists. They were the pole of attraction that spread the mobilization, as well as at the same time they were the object of the brutal repression by the forces of the state. Understanding these phenomena at the time of their occurrence has been presented as one of the contemporary challenges (Valencia, 2021), in view of the current opportunity of social impact in the construction of a different vision of the country.

REFERENCES

Anzola, B. (1990). Desarrollo de la sociología en Colombia. Décadas 60 y 70. Trabajo de pregrado sociología. Universidad de la Salle.

Barbary, O., & Urrea, F. (2004). *Gente Negra: Dinámicas sociopolíticas en Cali y el Pacífico*. Editorial Lealon.

Blair, E. (2005). La violencia frente a los nuevos lugares y/o los "otros" de la cultura. *Nueva antropología, 20*(65), 13–28. http://www.scielo.org.mx/scielo.php?script=sci_arttext&pid=S0185-06362005000200002&lng=es&tlng=es

Camacho, A., & Guzmán, A. (1990). *Colombia: ciudad y violencia*. Ediciones Foro Nacional.

Comisión de estudios sobre la violencia. (1987). *Colombia: violencia y democracia*. Universidad Nacional de Colombia.

Correa, A. (2016). *Sociología desde el caribe colombiano. Mirada de un sentipensante* (J. Vega, Comp.). Universidad del Norte.

Espinosa, A. (2011). De lo global a lo local en los repertorios de acción de las organizaciones negras frente al conflicto armado en Buenaventura. *Revista CS, 7*(7), 81–120.

Fals, O. (1955). *Peasant society in the Colombian Andes: a sociological study of the Saucio.* University of Florida Press.

Fals, O. (1980). La ciencia y el pueblo: nuevas reflexiones sobre la investigación-acción. In *La sociología en Colombia. Balance y perspectivas* (pp. 149–174). Bogotá. Colciencias.

Fals, O. (2002). *Historia doble de la Costa.* Universidad Nacional de Colombia. Banco de la República. El Ancora.

García, M. A. (2018). Contribución de las mujeres en las revistas de sociología colombianas 1959–2000. *Campos En Ciencias Sociales, 6*(1), 73–90. https://doi.org/10.15332/s2339-3688.2018.0001.03

Gilman, C. (2003). *Entre la pluma y el fusil. Debates y dilemas del escritor revolucionario en América Latina.* Siglo XXI.

Guzmán, G., Fals, B., & O. & Umaña, E. (1962). *La violencia en Colombia.* UN.

Jaramillo, J., Mora, L., & Cubides, F. (1986). *Colonización, coca y guerrilla.* UN.

Jaramillo Marín, J. (2011). Expertos y comisiones de estudio sobre la violencia en Colombia. *Estudios Políticos, 39,* 231–258. https://revistas.udea.edu.co/index.php/estudiospoliticos/article/view/11762

Leal, F., & Zamosc, L. (1990). *Al filo del caos: crisis política en la Colombia de los años 80.* Tercer Mundo.

Lynn, S. (1944). *Tabio, estudio de la organización social rural.* Minerva.

Molano, A. (1985). *Los años del tropel: relatos de violencia.* Cinep.

Molano, A. (1989). *Siguiendo el corte: relatos de guerras y de tierras.* Cinep.

Molano, A. (1994). *Trochas y fusiles.* Bogotá.

Molano, A., & Reyes, A. (1980). *Los bombardeos en el Pato.* Cinep.

Obregón, D. (1987). Sociología: de la palabra al concepto (una hipótesis sobre la constitución de la sociología como ciencia en Colombia). *Revista Colombiana de Sociología, 5*(1), 71–78. https://revistas.unal.edu.co/index.php/recs/article/view/8656/9300

Pécaut, D. (1998). La contribución del IEPRI a los estudios sobre la violencia en Colombia. *Análisis Político, 34,* 71–88. https://revistas.unal.edu.co/index.php/anpol/article/view/78900

Pizarro, E. (1996). *Insurgencia sin revolución. La guerrilla en Colombia en una perspectiva comparada.* Tercer Mundo.

Rappaport, J. (2021). *El cobarde no hace historia.* Universidad del Rosario.

Restrepo, G. (2002). *Peregrinación en pos de omega: sociología y sociedad en Colombia.* UN.

Rey, E. (2000). *El Carnaval, la segunda vida del pueblo.* Editorial Plaza & Janes.

Reyes, A. (1992). *Pacificar la paz: lo que no se ha negociado en los acuerdos de paz / Comisión de Superación de la Violencia.* Instituto de Estudios Políticos y

Relaciones Internacionales de la Universidad Nacional de Colombia, Comisión Andina de Juristas.

Rudas, N. (2019). Confrontación y "autodestrucción" de un proyecto de sociología en la Universidad Nacional de Colombia: la caída de los "padres fundadores". *Revista Colombiana de Sociología*, *42*(2), 67–90. https://doi.org/10.15446/rcs.v42n2.76759

Sánchez, G. (2004). El inacabado proceso de formación de un historiador. In A. Camacho (Ed.), *Artesanos y disciplinas. Hacer ciencias humanas en Colombia* (pp. 35–47). CESO.

Torres, C. (1961). *La proletarización de Bogotá: Ensayo de metodología estadística.* Fac. Sociología UN.

Uricoechea, F. (2001). La sociología en Colombia: Vocación, disciplina, profesión e historia. *Revista Colombia de sociología*, *6*(1), 17–25. https://revistas.unal.edu.co/index.php/recs/article/view/11048

Valencia, A. (2015). *La obra sociológica del profesor Álvaro Camacho Guizado (1939–2011).* Universidad del Valle – Universidad de los Andes.

Valencia, A. (2021). Qué está pasando en Colombia? Poder, legitimidad y crisis social. In A. Valencia et al. (Eds.), *Pensar la resistencia: mayo del 2021 en Cali y Colombia.* Cali Universidad del Valle.

Vega, D. R. (2012). Sobre historia y sociología: interdisciplinariedad y narración en las ciencias sociales en Colombia. *Anuario Colombiano de Historia Social y de la Cultura*, *39*(1), 243–262. https://www.redalyc.org/articulo.oa?id=127124561009

INTERVIEWS

Adriana Espinosa. November 2022. Bogota.
Alanis Bello. March 2022. Virtual.
Alba Ruano. May–June 2021. Virtual.
Aldemar Macias. March–April – 2022. Virtual.
Betty Ruth Lozano. March 2022. Bogota.
Blas de Zubiría. March 2021. Virtual.
Edgar Rey Sinnin. May. June 2021. Virtual.
Eduardo Pizarro Leongómez. March 2022. Bogotá.
Fernando Urrea. June 2021. Virtual.
Gloria Restrepo. February 2002. Bogotá.
Gloria Rivas. June 2021. Virtual.
Jaime Eduardo Jaramillo. June 2021. Virtual.
Magdalena León. March 2022. Bogotá.
Miguel Angel Beltrán. May 2021. Virtual.
Nohra Segura. December 2021. Virtual.
Olga Restrepo. June 2021. Virtual.

CHAPTER 6

Final Considerations

Abstract The conclusions provide an overview of the preceding chapters. In addition to opening the discussion on what particular processes of historicization imply, with differentiated emphasis on institutions, agents or situations, some critical points for sociological work in the country are also provided. Thus, what remains open is a possible research agenda that reflects the concerns of those who today practice sociology in Colombia.

Keywords History of sociology • Colombian sociologists • Intellectual diversity

In 2019 we celebrated 60 years of sociology in Colombia. This date refers to the creation of the first university training programs, a phenomenon associated with the full awareness acquired by a group of people, of the need to open and consolidate spaces for the academic and research development of the discipline. Sociologists' Day is celebrated on December 10. This refers to a speech given in 1882 in which a "new science" was presented, encouraging its extension in the applied studies that would allow the construction of a national project.

Of these two dates, 1959 can be taken as a starting point to give an account of the process of configuration of the field of sociology in Colombia, along with what this entails: the formation of a body of

J. Aldana Cedeño, *Sociology in Colombia*, Sociology Transformed, https://doi.org/10.1007/978-3-031-39412-6_6

professionals, obtaining the resources needed to advance research, opening up spaces for debate and dissemination, setting up a thematic agenda, among other aspects that have allowed the identification of certain distinctive features, specific contours, of sociology in the area of social and human sciences.

The particular characteristics of this process are described in the preceding chapters. Here it is interesting to draw attention to others that were not addressed or sufficiently highlighted, with the aim of raising questions or concerns about the opportunities and obstacles to the professional exercise of sociology. The first of these has to do with the areas in which job performance can take place.

In the case of Colombia, one of the activities carried out permanently by the people who have dedicated themselves to this profession, in the different stages that sociology has gone through, is teaching in universities. In these institutions it is expected that the teaching, research, and service dimensions are sufficiently articulated. In the case of social sciences, the latter two are more relevant in the sense they can guarantee pertinent, rigorous, and appropriate teaching.

However, this tendency, in which much of the research in sociology, or at least that in which the production that is legitimized through publications, awards or events is recognized, is promoted among the teaching teams in charge of the programs, rather than in research centers, creates certain difficulties. On the one hand, in some institutions, the type of funding is established on the teachers' hired hours and during the academic period, significantly reducing the real time allocated for research. On the other hand, the demand for external resources generates enormous pressures, more so in people who perceive themselves as academics and not managers.

In this way, the chapter in which reference to the importance of cooperation networks for the institutionalization of sociology is made, provokes thought on the sources of funding to advance research, as well as in the partnerships that can be formed at national and international levels. The interest in strengthening the latter encourages joint work in working groups or research committees in bodies such as the Consejo Latinoamericano de Ciencias Sociales (Latin American Council of Social Sciences)—Clacso—or the Latin American Studies Association—Lasa, just to mention two that have been central to the Colombian sociologists.

Although university spaces have been fundamental in this configuration of the field of sociology, their centrality has taken out of sight the important activity carried out elsewhere: public and private entities, NGOs or foundations, United Nations specialized agencies, research, and study centers. Some of this appears at the moment of accounting for that production visible through the legitimating instances mentioned above. What is left out, and is yet to be recorded, is the vast labor done in the regions, through community work, as well as its links with other areas, as the artistic or environmental for example.

In addition to this under-reporting, attempts on association have also failed to integrate these activities. The Asociación Colombiana de Sociología, with its disarticulations and refoundations, summons mostly academics. Recfades—Red Colombiana de Facultades y Departamentos de Sociología (Colombian Network of Faculties and Departments of Sociology)—has been, in recent history, the organization in charge of the national congresses of sociology. It has not yet been possible to form an association to bring together groups and individuals with different backgrounds. These difficulties feed solitary work, precisely due to the obstacles for the formation of teams that can be maintained for longer periods.

Other matters to be investigated relate to education and professionalization opportunities. For obvious reasons, at the time of opening the first programs few people had high-level training in the discipline. They were the ones who first occupied the department directions and deaneries chairs. The following generations have had greater opportunities for postgraduate training amid growing student mobility to foreign universities. However, scholarships and other support resources remain weak, due to the same deficiency of the science and technology system in the country.

In Colombia there is also an enormous gap between public and private education. In the former, there is a shortage of places to study and in the latter, costs hinder access. However, the presence of sociology in both areas has allowed the expansion of the discipline, especially due to the possibilities of expanding regional studies. In the regions, public universities have bet most on the presence of sociology. From there, research around the history of sociology in Colombia has also been promoted in recent years, largely concentrated so far in Bogota with the department of the Universidad Nacional de Colombia. Scholarly production for the case of Antioquia is remarkable, but it is still quite lacking in relation to other experiences.

To conclude, it is important to make a new reference to some of the topics that appear in the last chapter: what making sociology in a country that has suffered a prolonged armed conflict means and the place of women along with the transformations of sociological work, its theoretical and methodological orientation, in relation to new perspectives of analysis. On the first, the predominance of violence(s) as an object of study was already noted. Its addressing has been fundamental to understand the conflict and contribute to the processes of overcoming it and not repeating it. Surely this is an issue that will remain central in the research agenda because unfortunately it is a sustained situation in the country. However, it is necessary to expand this agenda that sometimes promotes endogamous practices. One of the sociologists interviewed questioned herself about the predominant readings from the suffering perspective, wondering if it is possible to also talk about pleasure and enjoyment. This sociologist has held, among other positions, as a researcher at the Centro Nacional de Memoria Histórica (National Center for Historical Memory), that is, she has also had to contribute to the construction of the memory of the conflict.

From this discussion, another follows. Although sociologists have been involved in state institutions, their participation in the same conflict has meant that, during certain periods, the exercise of the profession becomes dangerous. Some cases of persecution, imprisonment, disappearance, exile, and murder have already been mentioned, which are actually few in comparison to overall existing numbers. Fieldwork and community accompaniment in organizational processes have carried this risk for both social scientists and participants involved in these processes.

Regarding the second topic, the history of sociology in Colombia recognizes the founding fathers. Along with them, their wives, who in addition to this condition were also researchers, teachers, consultants and held managerial positions, appear. Among the investigations of Maria Cristina Salazar or Virginia Gutiérrez, are their contributions to the fields of family studies or child labor, problems that for a time were considered mainly female concerns.

Representativeness of women is low according to their own research trajectories. In many of the interviews with them, with a sample that covers several generations, the difficulties of trying to advance a work in equal conditions when there are factors, such as motherhood, which is not contemplated when constructing conditions of possibility, are recognized. At the same time, being a woman or being a trans woman implies facing different challenges when undertaking fieldwork, especially when it is carried out in conflict zones.

With it all, it is interesting to present a claim for a sociology whose results do not derive only in articles or books, but rather result in alternative practices, coherent and consistent with the accompaniment and transformations that are sought both in the communities in which it is present, and at the level of atavistic social structures that sustain inequality, injustice and, again, violence.

In closing, the reflections here presented can contribute to the purpose of continuing studies on sociological work in a comparative perspective. An important step in this direction has already been taken in current scholarship. For the Colombian case, the Chilean experience has allowed us to glimpse several points of convergence. The review of the trajectories followed in Argentina, Brazil and Mexico has allowed us to go in the same direction. I hope that works like this can continue to expand analysis questions beyond national borders.

Index[1]

[1] Note: Page numbers followed by 'n' refer to notes.

© The Author(s), under exclusive license to Springer Nature Switzerland AG 2023

J. Aldana Cedeño, *Sociology in Colombia*, Sociology Transformed, https://doi.org/10.1007/978-3-031-39412-6

93

9 783031 394119